PANZERS
AT WAR

PANZERS AT WAR

A. J. Barker

IAN ALLAN Publishing

First published 1978
This impression 1998

ISBN 0 7110 2578 9 (UK)
ISBN 1-55068-048-X (Canada)

Published by Ian Allan Publishing

an imprint of Ian Allan Ltd, Terminal House, Station Approach,
Shepperton, Surrey TW17 8AS.
Printed by Ian Allan Printing Ltd at its works at Coombelands in
Runnymede, England.

Published in North America and Canada by
Vanwell Publishing Ltd, St Catharines, Ontario.

Code: 9804/A2

Contents

Acknowledgements
The author is indebted to all those former
members of Wehrmacht who have helped
to make this book possible. In particular
thanks go to an old friend, Generalmajor
(aD) H. J. Löser and to Generalmajor
Horst Scheibert. All unacknowledged
photographs should be credited to
Bundesarchiv.

'Whenever in future wars the battle is fought,
panzer troops will play the decisive role ...'

Heinz Guderian
General der Panzertruppe
'Achtung Panzer!'

One face of war: A
panzergrenadier, whose
expression reflects the tension of
battle. This photograph was
taken during the 900 day siege of
Leningrad./*Podzun Verlag*

Foreword

Generalmajor a.D Hans-Joachim Löser

In 1939 the Wehrmacht's panzers were an untried and unproven weapon. To some senior German officers they were expensive toys, useful only as mobile batteries to support the sort of infantry attacks which had been a costly feature of World War I. But there were other far-sighted officers: notably Heinz Guderian and Erwin Rommel — both infantry officers — who had studied the theories propounded by Fuller and Liddell Hart in Britain, and who believed that the panzers should have a more independent role. In the event this led to a new kind of mobile warfare and spelled the end of the positional battles which had been the feature of 1914-1918. Movement triumphed over fire.

The campaign in Poland justified these ideas and the devastating potential of fast-moving armoured formations was recognised. Subsequently — in France and the Low Countries, in Russia and in North Africa — whenever the panzers were employed imaginatively and boldly they were a decisive factor in the land battle. Despite developments in anti-tank weapons they are likely to remain so in any major conflict in the foreseeable future. If only for this reason the publication of *Panzers at War* is particularly apt. For the *quantity*, if perhaps not the quality, of tanks with which Warsaw Pact armies are now equipped is vastly superior to the numbers which could be deployed by NATO.

Like my friend the author, I was a young infantry officer in 1939; like Colonel Barker also I have come to appreciate the tremendous importance and the current potential of armour — be it German, British, American or Soviet. In my view therefore this book is both important and instructive because today for technological reasons there is — as in 1939 — considerable discussion as to whether the tank is still 'King of the battlefield'.

Forging the Weapon

PzKpfw III. Autumn 1943.

Above: Wehrmacht manoeuvres 1937. PzKpfw Is and IIs deployed with horse cavalry.
/ *Generalmajor H. J. Löser*

'As I watched our formidable armoured column take off I began to understand the powerful impression our long columns of Panzers must have made at the beginning of the war, when they invaded the countries they still occupied. It was getting dark when we started to advance and the exhausts of the roaring masses of tanks flamed as they gathered speed and passed our heavy trucks, spreading out fanwise across the terrain. We felt curiously moved and stirred by the sight...'

Panzerjäger Oberleutnant Hals describing an action near Kharkov.

Between the two World Wars a number of far-sighted German officers studied ways and means of rectifying the short-comings which in 1918 had stopped their offensives just short of victory. The tank, they concluded, probably provided the answer. Tanks could smash a way through the enemy defence lines, and once they were through there was no limit to the havoc they could create. The snag was that by the terms of the Versailles Treaty Germany was forbidden to have tanks, or indeed any other form of strategic weapon. It seemed therefore that there was no way the tank enthusiasts could test their theories, and in the early 1930s men like Heinz Guderian — the most celebrated of these enthusiasts and subsequently the creator of the *Panzertruppe* — were forced to improvise experimental manoeuvres. Using motor cars carrying plywood dummies of tank turrets, they evolved a new philosophy of mechanised warfare, unsuspected by their past and future enemies and by no means easily accepted by their colleagues in the German General Staff.

The situation changed when the Nazis came to power in 1933. Hitler rejected the controls the Versailles Treaty imposed on German rearmament and backed his encouragement of arms production by making a considerable amount of money available to the armaments industry. But it takes a long time to acquire the industrial know-how and the requisite factory plant to produce armoured vehicles in quantity — despite the fact that General Hans Seekt, Commander-in-Chief of the German Army in the late 1920s and early 1930s, had negotiated an arrangement with the Russians by which secret German experimental and training establishments were set up in the Soviet Union. What the Germans learned in these establishments gave them valuable experience which enabled them to cut corners when they openly began to rearm in 1935. (From the Russian point of view it was also a worthwhile arrangement, as it was a means of acquiring the modern technologies and manufacturing processes of the long-established German military-industrial complex.)

By the mid-thirties the German Army, the Wehrmacht, was a formidable fighting force but it did not have either the right sort of equipment — or even enough of what there was — for the sort of operations envisaged by Guderian. Nevertheless when the war began in September 1939 the Germans enjoyed a technical superiority in tank design and construction which they were able to maintain throughout the war, despite intense efforts by the British, Americans and Russians to catch up. Thanks to Guderian's technical studies and his tactical exercises with the plywood chariots the Germans were also way ahead of every other country in the doctrine of the 'blitz'.

A Panzer Command was created in the summer of 1934 with the first *General der Panzertruppen*, Oswald Lutz, at its head and Guderian as Chief of Staff. In October the following year the first three panzer divisions were formed — without tanks, because there were only enough of the first light tanks, the PzIs, to equip one battalion. Furthermore the men to man the tanks when they did become available still had to be trained. On paper each of these three divisions was to have two tank regiments of two battalions, and a brigade of motorised infantry with field and anti-tank artillery batteries. Thus with engineers and signal companies, plus a motor-cycle battalion for reconnaissance duties, the new panzer division constituted a formidable all-arms battle group. In practice, however, the picture was different. The tanks were a long time coming from the factories and for nearly two years the divisions had only a handful of the 561 PzIs or PzIIs they were supposed to have. Moreover the die-hards who had opposed the formation of the *Panzertruppe* were still arguing that the tank was nothing more than an auxiliary weapon for the infantry. Guderian summed up the situation when he asked 'Do we want to destine panzer troops for close co-operation with the infantry or to use them for enveloping and outflanking operations in the open field? Do we want, if we are forced into a defensive war, to seek a rapid decision on the ground by large-scale, co-ordinated employment of the major striking force, or do we want to forego its inherent capacity for fast long-range movement, chain it to the slow tempo of infantry and artillery warfare, and so abandon from the start all hope of achieving a rapid decision of the battle and the war?'

The answer seemed obvious and once Guderian had defined the tank as a decisive weapon the success of the German *Panzertruppe* was a certainty. Nevertheless, it was a long time before his views were accepted and his plans translated into action. The German High Command — General Beck, Chief of the General Staff, in particular — remained sceptical, and was chary of employing tanks in large-scale operations in depth. Over and over again Guderian and the others who believed that armoured troops were the 'architects of victory', had to press their arguments in favour of the bold employment of tanks en masse. Guderian and his colleagues knew that their opposite numbers in France, Britain and Russia favoured the idea of using tanks in penny packets as infantry escorts, and the essence of their plan was concentrated attacks by large independent formations of panzers on a narrow front. One of Beck's arguments in response was that nobody had ever tried such tactics ever before.

The opportunity to do so in a small way presented itself with the outbreak of the Spanish Civil War. The Germans supported Franco's troops by providing German armoured vehicles, artillery and aircraft, and the German 'instructors' who manned them gained useful combat experience. Vehicles were in too short supply to practise concentrated attacks

and breakthrough techniques, but methods to co-ordinate the co-operation of tanks and aircraft were developed, tested and polished. In the summer of 1939 the annexation of Czechoslovakia yielded a useful bonus by way of 400 Czech army tanks, and production lines from which the Czech tanks continued to roll. With new German designations these tanks were enrolled in the service of the Reich and boosted the strength of Guderian's under-equipped and still expanding *Panzertruppe*.

At the beginning of September 1939 there were only five panzer divisions and by the end of the year there were but ten. This was well below the number which Guderian had said was necessary if victory was to be assured. Furthermore, although the German now had more than 3,000 tanks in service or in reserve, all but 300 were of the light PzIs and IIs. But the *Panzertruppe* had something which the British, French and Russian armies never acquired in so full a measure — specially selected and superbly trained men. Only the most promising recruits were allotted to the panzer divisions. Then, from the very start of their training, they were instilled with a fiercely professional pride and encouragement — not least by their dramatic black uniforms — to think of themselves as the Wehrmacht's élite. Every man was expected to master at least two of the basic trades of the panzer soldier — driver, gunner, radio operator — and the bloodless invasion of Czechoslovakia exercised many of them in operational procedure under semi-active service conditions.

Above: PzKpfw IIs. Their main armament was a 20mm heavy machine gun and they were never intended for tank-to-tank combat. Neither the PzIIs nor the PzIs had armour which would stand up to direct hits from field artillery or the anti-tank weapons in existence in 1939. But they were far removed from the 'cardboard' tanks with which the armchair experts in the West claimed Hitler's divisions were equipped.
/ *Generalmajor H. J. Löser*

The Early Panzers

Left and below: Developed by Krupp under the code name *Landwirtschaft-schlepper* (agricultural tractor) the PzKpfw I was built primarily as a training panzer but was employed in the Polish campaign and in the assault on the West in 1940. Armed only with two machine guns its chassis was used later in ammunition carriers, a few self-propelled guns, and command vehicles (*Panzerbefehlswagen*).

Top right: Surplus chassis from the production lines of the PzKpfw I were used as the basis of various armoured vehicles — including stop-gap self-propelled guns. This one is a 150mm Infantry gun (sIG 33) of the 1st Panzer Division photographed somewhere in the Balkans.

Bottom right: PzKpfw 35(t). One of the types of Czech tanks taken over by the Wehrmacht in 1939. The upper illustration shows one of these panzers on the Western Front in September 1939; the second photograph, which was taken in Russia in 1941, shows the divisional sign of the 6th Panzer Division.

Panzerkampfwagen I (PzKpfw I)

This tank, the 'Father of all Panzers' was the Wehrmacht's first armoured fighting vehicle and the machine which converted Adolf Hitler to the idea of panzer warfare.

Modifying the design of the British Carden-Loyd light tank of the 'thirties, the firm of Krupp built 150 vehicles which were issued to the Wehrmacht as *PzKpfw I Ausführung A* ('*Ausf.A*') (Model A). More of them were ordered until there were enough to equip the first three panzer divisions. A few saw action in the Spanish Civil War. Subsequently, when more sophisticated tanks were available, some PzKpfw Is were fitted out as tank destroyers and others equipped as command vehicles.

Characteristics of PzKpfw I Ausf. B
Weight: 6 tonnes
Length of hull: 4.02m
Width: 2.06m
Height: 1.72m
Crew: 2
Thickest armour: 13mm
Engine: 100hp Mayback 6-cylinder
        water cooled
Maximum (road) speed: 40kmph
Maximum range: 170km
Armament: 2 × 7.92mm MGs (MG30s)

Panzerkampfwagen 35(t) and Panzerkampfwagen 38(t) (PzKpfw35(t) and PzKpfw38(t))

When the Germans occupied Czechoslovakia in 1939 the Czech Army had two tanks in service. The first, known as the LTM 35 and produced by Skoda, had a high silhouette, riveted armour and unsatisfactory suspension. However 167 of these vehicles were taken into service by the Wehrmacht (most of them went to the 6th Panzer Division) and re-named the PzKpfw 35(t). Their chassis were used later for artillery ammunition carriers and tractors.

The other Czech tank, the TNHP-8, which had a Christie-type suspension, was a more satisfactory vehicle and the Germans adopted it as the PzKpfw 38(t). With minor modifications it continued to roll off the production lines until 1942; at one period in 1940 a quarter of German tanks were Kpfw38(t)s. Subsequently the hull became the basis of a number of self-propelled guns such as the Marder III.

Characteristics of the Kpfw35(t)
Weight: 10.5 tonnes
Crew: 4

13

Left: A Marder III SP gun in Normandy during 1944. On the right of the road is the wing of an Allied glider.

Below: PzKpfw 38(t). This, the second type of Czech tank, saw considerable service and when it was superseded by the PzKpfw III in 1942 its hull was used for various self-propelled guns such as the Marder III and later the *Hetzer Jagdjäger.* Between 1944 and 1945 the chassis of the 38(t) was also used in flame-throwing panzers and as the basis of a panzer recovery vehicle, the *Bergepanzer.*

Thickest armour: 25mm
Engine: 120hp (Praga 6-cylinder, water
    cooled)
Maximum (road) speed: 35kmph
Armament: 1 × 37mm KwK gun,
       1 × 7.92mm MG

Characteristics of the Kpfw38(t)
Weight: 9.73 tonnes
Length (of hull): 4.9m
Width: 2.06m
Height: 2.37m
Crew: 4
Thickest armour: 25mm
Engine: 125hp (Praga 6-cylinder, water
    cooled)
Maximum road/cross
   country speed: 42/15kmph
Maximum range: 230km
Armament: 1 × 37mm KwK gun,
       1 × 7.92mm MG

Panzerkampfwagen II (PzKpfw II)

According to General Heinz Guderian in his book *Panzerführer** the PzKpfw II tank was a stop-gap vehicle — welcome only because the appearance of the more efficient PzKpfw IIIs and PzKpfw IVs was delayed. Manufacture of the Kpfw II was entrusted to the MAN *(Maschinenfabrik-Augsburg-Nürnberg)* Company and production started in 1935. Several models, each an improvement on its predecessor were built and in the French campaign of 1940 the Wehrmacht had 955 tanks of this type. Plans were laid for 1,067 Kpfw IIs to come off the assembly line in 1941 but the number was reduced to 860.

Although the PzKpfw II was fast and had a good cross-country performance, its 20mm gun was of little use against the armour of most enemy tanks, and its own armour was little protection against anything more than close-range small arms fire and shell splinters.

Characteristics of PzKpfw II Ausf.D
Weight: 10 tonnes
Crew: 3
Thickest armour: 30mm
Engine: 140hp Mayback 6-cylinder,
      water cooled
Maximum road/cross
  country speed: 55/19kmph
Armament: 20mm KwK 30 and
      2 × 7.92mm MGs

**Panzerführer* (Panzer Leader) Michael Joseph, London 1953.

Above: PzKpfw II.

Below left: PzKpfw IIs in France in 1940. Ausf.B has its frontal armour increased to 30mm. Ausf.C had an improved suspension. This 'mark' constituted the backbone of the panzer divisions during 1940 and it was still in service in 1942.

Blitzkrieg in Poland

The invasion of Poland, where the *Panzertruppen* were blooded in near ideal conditions, gave the Wehrmacht commanders an opportunity to gain experience in the handling of mechanised and motorised formations. Up to then nobody had been able to foresee how the new weapon would stand up to actual combat conditions.

The disparity in total forces committed was not great, but in armour it was astronomical. To counter the 3,000 tanks of the six panzer divisions which the Germans threw into the attack, the Poles could field only two tank brigades with a total of about 500 armoured vehicles dating from World War I or shortly after. They had very few effective anti-tank weapons and their air force and anti-tank defences were quite inadequate. As Poland is generally flat, with no major physical obstacles to deter an armoured advance, in the dry autumn weather of

September 1939 it was excellent terrain for tanks. Spearheading the invasion the panzer divisions slashed through the thin screen of six Polish armies like knives through butter. The Poles fought with futile gallantry. (Oddly enough there was not a single direct encounter between German and Polish tanks throughout the whole campaign, but horse cavalry charged German tanks on several occasions and Polish gunners invariably fought to the end). In a few days, however, they were rolled up in several clusters, each completely surrounded and without any overall direction. It was all over inside four weeks; crucified by the Wehrmacht and the Red Army together, Poland lay at the mercy of the invaders, and one by one the Polish islands of resistance succumbed. Warsaw, facing starvation and typhoid, fell, and Germany and Russia divided the country between themselves while the German

Below: A PzKpfw II of the 4th Panzer Division in a Warsaw street on 13 September 1939. For the Polish anti-tank gunners, who were dug into the rubble left after days of bombing by the Luftwaffe, these panzers were sitting ducks, and in three hours the 4th Division lost 57 of the 120 tanks they committed to the battle.

Above: 3 September 1939: PzKpfw Is and IIs in Poland. These were units commanded by Guderian — standing in the command vehicle on the right. The loose black berets or *Schutzmütze* worn by the tankmen were withdrawn in the winter of 1939/40 and are now much sought after by collectors of German military headgear.

Left: The Sturmgeschütz III (SdKfz 142) or StuG III was one of the first German 'mobile assault guns' which was not a stop-gap weapon. Its chassis was that of the PzKpfw III, and the vehic'... itself was in effect a turretless tank, mounting a short 75mm L/24 gun with a limited traverse. Five prototypes took part in the campaign in France 1940, and the StuG III went into regular production in July of that year.

armies slowly recoiled to prepare for the next move against Western Europe.

It had been a whirlwind campaign, a spectacular demonstration of 'blitzkrieg', in which the panzers had shown that adherence to the old proven principles of war — offensive action, surprise, concentration of effort and mobility — still paid a handsome dividend. Fire and movement was the secret of the new warfare, and military experts all over the world could now see that given the right conditions the panzers were irresistible. Yet the technique they had employed was simple enough. Guderian's columns had

exploited weak spots and gaps in the Polish defence lines or simply driven round positions where the opposition was strong. In doing so they had often crossed country which Poles regarded as un-tankable. Only when they tried to burst through a heavily defended line by sheer gunpower, and to battle a way through the suburbs of Warsaw had they suffered heavy casualties. (In the first instance they invariably had to pull back while the infantry mounted set piece attacks; in the

Right: Inside the fighting compartment of a StuG III.

Below: The StuG III weighed only 24 tons and was easily ferried across rivers on the standard engineer pontoon equipment.

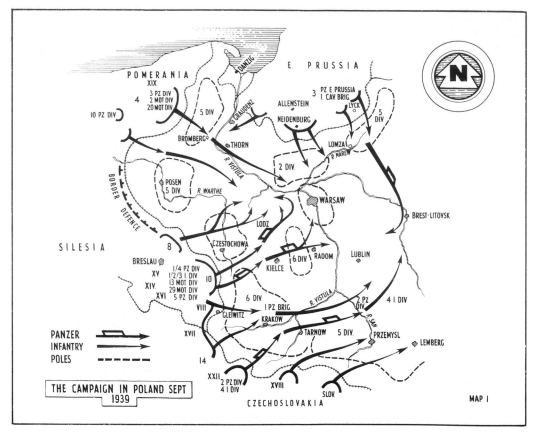

second they lost 57 out of 120 tanks to Polish anti-tank gunners, before it was appreciated that the tracks with which the panzers were then equipped were not suitable for street fighting.)

So long as they did not try to fight by the book — their speed and mobility gave the panzers a tremendous advantage in operations where the enemy was still following the rules of World War I. Time and again the panzers had upset the whole Polish defence plan, simply by driving round positions for which there would have been a heavy price to pay in blood and bones if a conventional assault had been necessary. As Guderian had predicted, the unexpected appearance of a single troop of tanks in the rear of the enemy's defences could create far more consternation than a whole battalion advancing from the front.

The secret of success appeared to lie in the panzers acting independently, with the infantry, the artillery, sappers and service troops being treated as auxiliaries. The trouble was that not all the German generals were willing to see things in this light, and there were to be many instances, right up to the end of the war, of panzer formations being split up and sometimes even placed under command of infantry. German infantrymen were singing *Die Infantrie, die Königin der Waffen* (Infantry, Queen of Arms) — a song that expressed the opinions of many

of their senior commanders — long after the Polish campaign.

Until he was conducted round the battlefields on 5 September, Hitler himself had never properly appreciated the potential of the panzers. Up to then he had shared Goering's view about the omnipotence of air power, and when he saw the first of a series of devastated Polish positions he asked 'Our Stukas did that?' Guderian's proud reply 'No! Our panzers', gave the Führer cause to reflect on his ideas. The panzers, he now realised, were a weapon which no other nation had exploited; the Luftwaffe had its limitations but panzers and Luftwaffe together could win for Germany all the *Lebensraum* she needed. Subsequently the rapid advance of the armoured columns to the gates of Warsaw and through the mountains in the south was to confirm Hitler's ideas.

Attempts were now made to correct the more obvious deficiencies in organisation, tactics and equipment. By virtue of its concept of mobility the panzer division had been designed to operate in open flat terrain, avoiding areas where vehicles could be ambushed and which would slow down the momentum of attack. So long as panzers stuck to the rules their successes in Poland showed that there was nothing wrong with the basic concept. But the tanks needed infantry support when they ran up against an obstacle which they could not circumvent. Many of the 217 tanks which had been knocked out in the campaign resulted from the fact that infantry support was not available when it was needed to sweep the opposition aside. The bulk of the infantry marching up to the battle front was too far behind, and the panzer's own panzergrenadiers were restricted by their soft-skinned trucks. Armoured infantry carriers which would enable the panzergrenadiers to keep right up with the tanks were needed. The agreed solution was to provide half-tracks, and the mobile infantry was issued with this type of vehicle throughout the war — but never fast enough; even in 1944 none of the panzer divisions was an armoured division in post-war terms.

Several formations which had taken part in what the General Staff was now calling the 'Great Manoeuvres' in Poland were judged to have failed in their purpose. Most of the approbium was heaped on the infantry — some of the German leaders saying that the wretched foot soldiers had failed to fight with the fervour of their forefathers. If it had not been for the Luftwaffe and the panzers, several of the generals claimed, the campaign would have been so slow that the French and British might have been tempted to launch an irresistible offensive. The horsed cavalry was an obvious candidate for the axe, although the cavalry section of the General Staff in Berlin actually put in a bizarre bid for an increase in its establishment. These efforts came to nothing; horses were outmoded the generals decided, and so the cavalry establishment was severely pruned (There was in fact to be a role for horsed cavalry in Russia later, but this was not foreseen in October 1939).

The gunners also came in for a share of recrimination. According to General Fedor von Bock, the commander of the army group which had converged from both sides of the Polish corridor, the artillery was immobile and far too slow in deploying its fire. The answer to this, said General Erich von Manstein, was motorised assault guns. And in due course the obsolescent PzKpfw I, rebuilt and fitted with a Czech field gun, became the first of these self-propelled 'assault' guns. The four so-called 'light' divisions — semi-mechanised hybrid formations with a few tanks — had not shown up well either, so they were converted to panzer divisions. In their place a new type of division the *panzergrenadier division* was created to operate in close country — the terrain which panzer divisions were

to avoid. (The difference between the panzer division and the panzergrenadier division was primarily the mix of vehicles. Where the panzer division had a large number of tanks and armoured cars, with a smaller complement of half-tracks for its infantry, the panzergrenadier division was the other way round.)

All the foregoing changes related to the employment of armoured formations on the battlefield. So far as equipment was concerned the 'Great Manoeuvres' offered little in the way of practical experience because hostile tanks had not clashed head-on as they did nine months later in France. Towards the end of the campaign, however, mechanical failure caused a number of tanks to drop out of action, and when the Poles surrendered nearly every German panzer needed overhauling. Concern was expressed, but conditions were reckoned to be exceptional. And with German factories now producing 125 tanks a month and the Czech production lines doing almost as well, it was agreed that the panzer force would expand rapidly. Thus, apart from any improvements in the design and quality of the tanks themselves, the experts were confident that in another campaign the deployment of more panzer divisions would ease the strain, and consequently the incidence of operational breakdowns would be reduced.

Above: Two of the first *Mittlerer Schützenpanzer-Wagen* (SPW — medium armoured personnel carrier). SdKfz 251 developed by Hanomag (Hannover Maschinenbau GmbH) this half-track troop carrier was designed to carry 10 men and their equipment. The chassis was also used for a variety of armoured superstructures, for ambulances, ammunition and supply vehicles and some artillery weapons. The first of them saw action in France, but the production did not permit a general issue until the start of the Russian campaign in 1941. This particular vehicle carries the registration of the Luftwaffe.

The Assault on the West

In Britain and France the successes of the panzers in the 'little war' with Poland produced only short-sighted reactions. On 5 October 1939 Hitler took the salute at a victory parade in Warsaw, and a film of the panzer divisions driving past the Führer was shown in the West. Some intelligence experts who saw this film dismissed it as propaganda, and the myth of the 'cardboard tanks' was perpetuated. Other experts concluded that although the speed of execution of the Polish campaign was almost unique, its outcome could be attributed to the Germans having slightly more modern equipment than the Poles. Not until the German offensive in the West produced similar results on an even bigger scale did the Western pundits begin to revise their ideas.

At the outset of what they called the Western Campaign the Germans had about 2,600 tanks of which 450 were of Czech origin and equipped with a 37mm gun. The majority were the light PzKpfw Is and PzKpfw IIIs mounting 37mm or 50mm guns, but there were also one or two of the new PzKpfw IVs which were equipped with 75mm cannons. On the Allied side, France could muster about 3,000 tanks — of which nearly half were deployed in light mechanised and armoured divisions, the remainder being dispersed among the infantry; and there were about 300 British tanks with the British Expeditionary Force (BEF). Of the latter 210 were light vehicles, the remainder were the new heavy Matildas; all were committed to infantry support. In the United Kingdom another 174 light

Below: A PzKpfw II bogged down on the Western Front in the hard winter of 1939/40.

Above: One of the first PzKpfw
IVs — also on the Western Front
1939/40.

Right: A PzKpfw IV in the
advance of May 1940...

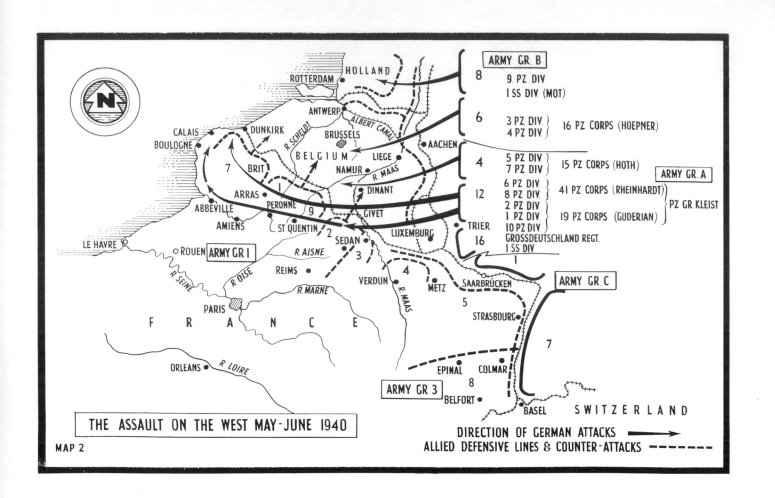

ARMY GR. B

8   9. PZ. DIV.
     I SS DIV. (MOT)

6   3 PZ. DIV. } 16 PZ CORPS (HOEPNER)
     4 PZ. DIV. }

4   5 PZ. DIV. } 15 PZ CORPS (HOTH)
     7 PZ. DIV. }   ARMY GR. A

12   6 PZ. DIV. } 41 PZ CORPS (RHEINHARDT)
     8 PZ. DIV. }
     2 PZ. DIV. } 19 PZ CORPS (GUDERIAN)   } PZ GR KLEIST
     1 PZ. DIV. }

16   10 PZ. DIV.
     GROSSDEUTSCHLAND REGT.
     I SS DIV.

ARMY GR. C

HOLLAND
ROTTERDAM
ANTWERP
R. SCHELDT
ALBERT CANAL
CALAIS
DUNKIRK
BOULOGNE
BRUSSELS
BELGIUM
AACHEN
LIEGE
NAMUR
R. MAAS
7
BRIT
1
DINANT
ARRAS
ABBEVILLE
PERONNE
9
GIVET
AMIENS
ST QUENTIN
2
LUXEMBURG
TRIER
LE HAVRE
ROUEN   ARMY GR I
SEDAN
R. AISNE
3
R. SEINE
R. OISE
REIMS
VERDUN
R. MAAS
METZ
SAARBRÜCKEN
5
R. MARNE
4
PARIS
STRASBOURG
F R A N C E
7
ORLEANS   R. LOIRE
EPINAL   COLMAR
ARMY GR. 3
8
BELFORT
BASEL   S W I T Z E R L A N D

THE ASSAULT ON THE WEST MAY-JUNE 1940

MAP 2

DIRECTION OF GERMAN ATTACKS ———→
ALLIED DEFENSIVE LINES & COUNTER-ATTACKS –––––

tanks and 156 'cruisers' were about to be shipped when the German offensive began. (They landed at Cherbourg on 22 May 1940 and were promptly sent into action — some before the crews had time to prepare them properly).

In effect, although the Allies could field nearly twice as many tanks as the Germans, they were caught napping. With the French frontier on the eastern flank hermetically sealed off by the Maginot Line, the Allies had expected the attack to be directed through Holland and northern Belgium, following the course of the old Schlieffen Plan of World War I. And indeed this was the Germans' original intention. But after Poland General von Manstein had suggested that a strong force of panzers should move through what the French had dubbed as the 'impassable' terrain in the Ardennes of southern Belgium, and move rapidly west and north to the coast. Meantime the Allies would be lured into the Low Countries by a secondary and conventional attack from the direction they were expecting the Germans to advance.

When this plan was translated into action in May 1940 it was completely successful. The French tanks were more heavily armoured than the panzers and their guns were more powerful; so too were the heavy Matildas with the British Expeditionary Force. But the Allies soon learned that the success of tanks does not always depend on the classic factor of protective armour or even more powerful armament. The French practice of the tank commander in the turret acting as gunner reduced the efficiency of their tanks, and British control procedures were far too complex and unwieldy. Not only were the panzers faster they were fitted with better radio equipment;

Below: ... and a PzKpfw III.

Right: PzKpfw III.

Below: This photograph appears to have been posed, but it was claimed to have been taken in June 1940. The vehicle is an unusual mobile anti-tank equipment — a PzKpfw I Ausf.B chassis with a 4.7mm Czech gun.

consequently they could be used more purposefully.

Teamwork, determination and the confident application of Guderian's catch phrase *'Klotzen, nicht Kleckern'* (Don't tickle with the fingers, hit with the fist) enabled the panzers to wreak havoc behind the Allied front. Within five weeks they had roared through to the Channel coast and a German victory was assured. The Allied armour was chopped into segments, each of which was dealt with in turn. The Germans exploited their air superiority to the full, and when the panzers engaged the Allied tanks they generally managed to do so with numerical superiority. Moreover, because the panzers had rampaged through the Allied rear areas, disrupting supplies and communications, the French and British vehicles often ran out of fuel and ammunition. The crews of the Allied tanks fought courageously and the outcome of many an engagement was settled solely by superiority of panzer techniques.

At a crucial period in the campaign when the French were in complete disorder and the BEF was retreating hot-foot towards the coast, three of Guderian's panzer divisions were within 15 miles of Dunkirk and poised to strike. Two motorised divisions were roaring up to join them, and behind them several infantry divisions were also marching up as fast as they could. The British were working furiously to organise the town's defences, but it was ripe for the taking next day. Only a direct order from Hitler to stop the advance saved the BEF. No-

Above: A 4-wheeled scout car in a Brussels street. This type of car normally mounted a 20mm cannon.

Top right: PzKpfw III of the 7th Panzer Division.

Centre right: Marder II classed as a 'tank hunter' (*Panzerjäger*). It was built on redundant PzKpfw II chassis and mounted a 75mm anti-tank gun.

Bottom right: A Marder II.

one has quite understood why the standstill order was given — although a number of explanations have been suggested, including Goering's wish to seize a slice of glory for the Luftwaffe. But the fact that the panzers were halted by the Fuhrer's intervention has left one of the biggest 'ifs' in history.

An armistice with the French was signed on 22 June and the *Panzertruppen* became the heroes of the hour. Guderian's force was credited with 250,000 prisoners in thirteen days of combat, and Hitler's enthusiasm for the panzers led to his demanding that tank production — then running at 125 per month — should be raised to 800 per month. To Guderian's dismay a campaign in Russia was firmly in prospect and the Führer's aim was to double the number of panzer divisions. When Dr Todt, the Minister of Armaments and War Production, finally convinced him that a programme of such magnitude could not be mounted overnight and that production of U-Boats and aircraft would be bound to suffer, Hitler ordered that the doubling of the panzer divisions should be effected by halving the number of tanks on the establishment of existing divisions,

(reducing the number to between 150 and 210). Quantity was to take precedence over quality, and the seeds of disaster were being sown.

Efforts were made to rectify some of the faults that had shown up in the recent campaign. The panzergrenadiers still needed cross-country personnel carriers, and orders were given for production to be accelerated of the 3-ton half-tracks which had been developed after the war in Poland. This, and the production of other vehicles for the new panzer and panzergrenadier divisions which were now being raised, coupled with the progressive motorisation of the rest of the Wehrmacht, put an additional strain on Germany's steel and motor industries. (It is ironic that the industries of the conquered nations could provide only limited assistance when they were finally harnessed to the German war effort, and very few of the thousands of captured vehicles were suitable for employment in the field). In the event more of the half tracks were built in Germany during the war than any other type of armoured vehicle. Although only 950 were built in 1941, some 7,800 rolled off the production lines in 1944.

Following an almost unanimous re-

commendation by the panzer generals, it was decided to withdraw the light PzKpfw Is and IIs, and replace them with PzKpfw IIIs and IVs. It was also decided to give the new tanks more powerful guns and thicken their armour. The guns and armour of the Matildas and the French Char Bs had both proved superior to the PzKpfw IVs, and it was logical to suppose that the panzers would be meeting even better tanks in the not too distant future. (Although it seems that little consideration was given to the Soviet tanks which were known to be under development.) The PzKpfw III underwent a programme of up-gunning with a short 50mm gun and the armour of the PzKpfw III and IV was increased.

It took time, of course, before the light tanks were replaced by the new ones, before the old mediums could be refurbished, and before the panzergrenadiers got their full complement of half-tracks. At the beginning of 1941 the reorganisation and re-equipping was far from complete. Nevertheless, taking into account their experience and confidence, the German panzer force had what amounted to a three year lead over Germany's current and future enemies.

29

Left and above: The *Wespe* (SP gun) also mounted on a PzII chassis, boasted a 105mm field gun-howitzer.

Maurice Few, a British Officer, was captured on 1 June 1940 near Godeswald by Rommel's 7th Panzer Division:

'I found his troops to be correct but courteous and without the arrogance we were to experience later. The entire division seemed to be dressed in brand new British Army battle dress trousers with a Wehrmacht jacket; many wore a gaily coloured silk scarf round their necks and had a tendency to long hair. I was told that everyone in the division was under 30 years old but no doubt this did not apply to Rommel and perhaps some of his div staff. Somebody silently presented me with a "hussif", presumably because my battle dress was in tatters. Someone else — obviously a panzer humorist — held out his clenched fists, one above the other. The upper fist was then vigorously pumped up and down while the lower fist remained stationary to the chant "Chemblin, Chemblin". (This was intended to take off Neville Chamberlain raising and lowering his famous umbrella.) . . .

. . . I noted an ingenious money saver. This was a "mechanized" field cooker which simply comprised a horsedrawn field cooker run up onto the back of a lorry and its wheels lashed to ring bolts. The cook stood on the back of the lorry cooking just as he would have been doing on the line of march when his cooker had been drawn by two heavy draft horses.

Maps throughout Rommel's division appeared to comprise Michelin tourist maps. They were bang up to date but, in so far as I can remember after this lapse of time, without grid co-ordinates. Nonetheless they were vastly preferable to our ordnance survey sheets dated 1924. All vehicles appeared to be fitted with Dunlop tyres and so did some grounded aircraft . . .'

Panzer Development

Panzerkampfwagen III (PzKpfw III (SdKfz 141))

The PzKpfw III, which was intended to be the Wehrmacht's main combat vehicle, was developed in the mid-thirties by Daimler Benz under the pseudonym *Zugführerwagen* (platoon commanders' truck). In 1940, when the French campaign opened, the Germans had 349 of them and the initial victories in Russia were made possible only because of the large numbers of Kpfw IIIs employed there. From the very beginning however the choice of armament was a matter of serious contention. A 37mm gun with a co-axial MG34 was mounted in the first models, (*Ausführungen* A, B, C, D and E : 'E' being the 1939 production model). But by 1940 it had been decided to upgun the tanks in service and to fit all future models with a 50mm gun. Orders were given for the 5cm L/42 gun to be fitted on models E, F, G and H, but on Hitler's insistence the more powerful L/60 5cm gun was fitted to all tanks from 1941 onwards (Ausf J-1) and to all re-conditioned vehicles.

Characteristics of the PzKpfw III Ausf. F (SdKfz 141)

Weight: 19.5 tonnes
Length of hull: 5.41m
Width: 2.92m
Height: 2.51m
Armour: 30mm, turret 30mm

Crew: 5
Maximum road/cross
  country speed: 40/18kmph
Maximum range: 175km
Armament: 1 × 50mm KwK L/60 or
  50mm L/42 and 1 × MG

5,650 PzKpfw IIIs of all types were manufactured during the years 1939-1943. The PzKpfw III was the standard German medium tank towards the beginning of the war. It saw action in practically every panzer battle of the war.

Far left, top: Panzers of Guderian's Group supported by infantry deploying for attack during the assault on the West in May 1940. The tank on the front left is a PzKpfw 35(t). On the right is a PzKpfw III — one of the early models armed with a 37mm gun.

Far left, centre: PzKpfw III in the Western Desert in 1943.

Far left, bottom: In Tunisia. This one has a 75mm KwK L/24 gun.

Left: At the central sector of the Russian front in 1944 — mounting a 50mm KwK L/60.

Below left: A *Hetzer* tank destroyer in the Balkans 1944.

Below: Front end of a *Hetzer* tank destroyer.

Above: The PzKpfw IV was originally designed as a medium support tank mounting a short 75mm howitzer. In the foreground is one of the early models on the Western Front in 1939. In the rear a PzKpfw III.

Centre right: Another of the early Kpfw IVs, fitted with the short 75mm L/24 howitzer — seen in Russia at the end of 1941.

Bottom right: The need for more powerfully armed medium tanks necessitated continued up-gunning and the PzKpfw IVs shown here mounted a long-barrelled 75mm anti-tank gun (KwK L/53).

Panzerkampfwagen IV (PzKpfw IV)

Under the code-name *Battalionsführerwagen* (Battalion Commander's vehicle) the PzKpfw IV was developed at the same time as the PzKpfw III, and the first production model, Ausf.A, appeared in 1936. Designed originally as an 'infantry' tank, and for a different tactical role from other panzers, its armour was thin but it carried a powerful 75mm gun which could match any other tank of that period. In subsequent models, B-E, the armour was thickened and in 1941 Ausf.F appeared. This tank, and the models (E-J) which followed, were able to take on the remarkable and outstanding Soviet T-34/76 on equal terms. But it was 1944 before the PzKpfw IVs with the L/48 guns came into production and by then the war had turned against Germany.

About 6,000 of the H and J models were produced between 1943 and the end of the war.

Because the chassis of the PzKpfw IV was extremely reliable and robust it was used for a wide variety of other panzer variants, the various assault guns being the most important.

Above: Photographed in France at the beginning of 1944 the PzKpfw IV shown was the final version. Note the skirting plates — protection against hollow charge infantry anti-tank weapons.

Characteristics of the PzKpfw IVA and IVJ

	IVA	IVJ
Weight:	17.3 tonnes	25 tonnes
Length of hull:	5.91m	5.89m (7.02 over gun)
Width:	2.86m	3.29m (over skirt armour)
Height:	2.68m	2.68m
Crew:	5	5
Thickest armour:	20mm	80mm
Engine:	250hp	300hp
Maximum road/cross country speed:	35/20kmph	40/16kmph
Maximum range:	200km	200km
Armament:	1 × 75mm KwK L/24 and 2 MGs	1 × 75mm KwK L/48 and 2 MGs

Right: The panzer in this photograph was one of those issued to the SS-Panzer Regiment 12, the *Hitlerjugend* Division.

Below: The *Brummbär* (Grizzly Bear) Sturmpanzer IV was a heavily armoured close support assault gun. The gun itself was a 150mm L/12 howitzer; the chassis was a variant of the PzIV. This *Brummbär* was photographed in Italy in 1944.

Left: The *Nashorn* (Rhinoceros) was a self-propelled anti-tank gun — mounting the ubiquitous 88mm PAK 43/1 L/71 gun on the chassis of a PzIV. This photograph taken on the central sector of the Russian front early in 1944 suggests that the horse still had a communications role in a country of few roads and a shortage of PoL.

Centre right: The *Jagdpanzer* (Hunter tank) *Hummel* was a 150mm *Panzerfeldhaubitze 18M* (sFH18) gun-howitzer on a PzKpfw III or PzKpfw IV chassis. The photograph was taken in the Ukraine in 1943 and shows the *Hummel* on a PzIV chassis.

Bottom right: A 150mm gun on the *Hummel*.

North Africa and the Balkans

While the Wehrmacht was preparing for the attack on Russia two digressions supervened; both stemmed from the need to pull Mussolini's chestnuts out of the fire. The 5th Light Division — a mechanised and partially armoured division — and the 15th Panzer Division had to be sent to Libya in February 1941 to bolster the failing Italians, who had just been thrashed by a small British armoured force. Two months later Hitler reluctantly ordered an invasion of Yugoslavia and Greece to strengthen Germany's southern flank, which had become vulnerable due to the failure of Italy's invasion of Greece. These major diversions, combined with a multitude of minor commitments, sapped the strength of the forces destined for the conquest of Russia and made impossible the total concentration on the greatest military operation in history.

North Africa

Lieut General Erwin Rommel was appointed to command the German forces in North Africa and within two months of his arrival he had bundled the British out of all the territory they had captured. Looping and wheeling around the British positions the panzers exploited every opportunity to the full. Their tactics were bold and unorthodox and the man who directed them was soon being called 'the Desert Fox'. For the next eighteen months Rommel and a succession of British generals sparred with one another up and down the Western Desert. This imaginative panzer leader sometimes took unjustifiable risks, but they generally paid dividends. The Germans had better equipment — though never enough of it — and they extracted the maximum adantage from their panzers, their anti-tank guns and the magnificent 88mm anti-aircraft guns they used in a ground role.

Rommel stuck faithfully to the blitzkrieg creed and Guderian's principle of *'Klotzen nicht Kleckern'* — keeping his panzers concentrated and employing them to achieve massive local superiority at the decisive moment; they were never frittered away in pointless battles of attrition. To the British troops the Desert Fox became a sort of bogy-man, an invisible will-o'-the-wisp whose panzers had a habit of suddenly appearing from nowhere — and disappearing equally quickly. And this psychological ad-

Below: PzKpfw III.

Left: PzKpfw III.

Below: North Africa early 1943. German 8-wheeled Armoured Car SdKfz 231, with the early type frame radio-aerial, captured by British troops.

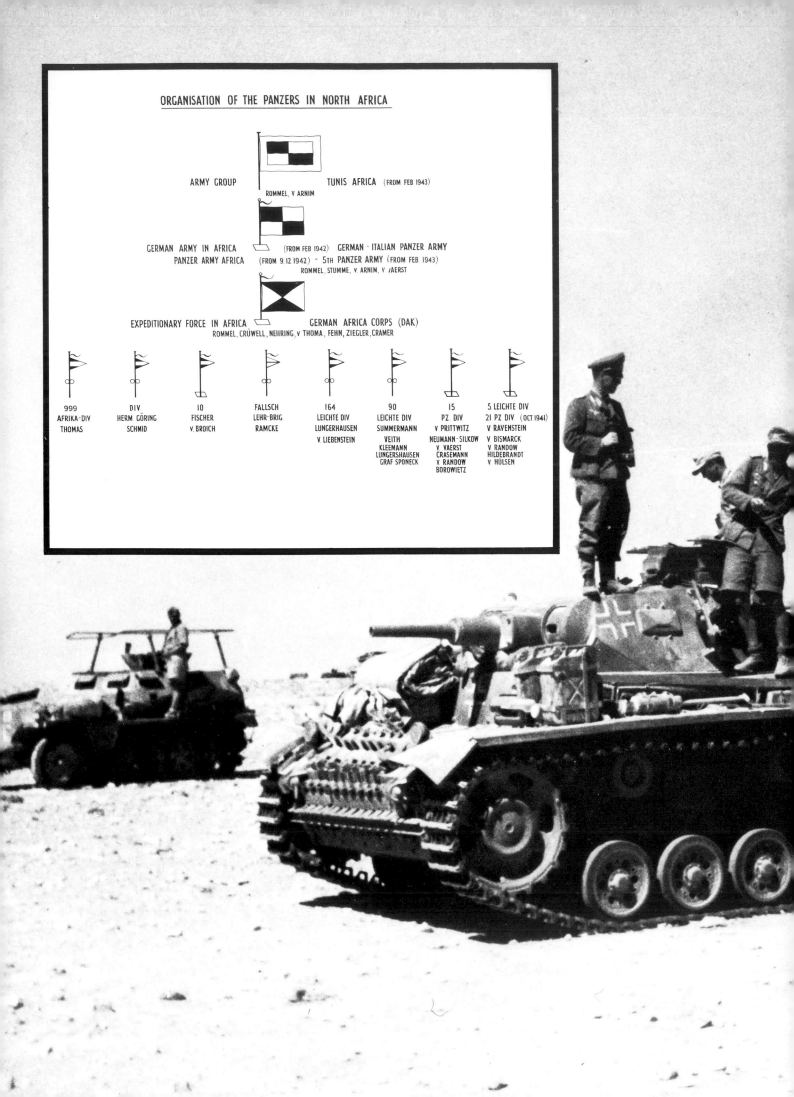

ORGANISATION OF THE PANZERS IN NORTH AFRICA

ARMY GROUP   TUNIS AFRICA (FROM FEB 1943)

ROMMEL, V ARNIM

GERMAN ARMY IN AFRICA   (FROM FEB 1942)   GERMAN - ITALIAN PANZER ARMY
PANZER ARMY AFRICA   (FROM 9.12.1942) - 5TH PANZER ARMY (FROM FEB 1943)

ROMMEL, STUMME, V. ARNIM, V VAERST

EXPEDITIONARY FORCE IN AFRICA   GERMAN AFRICA CORPS (DAK)

ROMMEL, CRÜWELL, NEIIRING, V THOMA, FEHN, ZIEGLER, CRAMER

| 999 AFRIKA-DIV THOMAS | DIV HERM GÖRING SCHMID | 10 FISCHER v. BROICH | FALLSCH LEHR-BRIG RAMCKE | 164 LEICHTE DIV LUNGERHAUSEN v. LIEBENSTEIN | 90 LEICHTE DIV SUMMERMANN VEITH KLEEMANN LUNGERSHAUSEN GRAF SPONECK | 15 PZ DIV v PRITTWITZ NEUMANN-SILKOW v. VAERST CRASEMANN v. RANDOW BOROWIETZ | 5 LEICHTE DIV 21 PZ DIV (OCT 1941) v RAVENSTEIN v. BISMARCK v. RANDOW HILDEBRANDT v HÜLSEN |

vantage was enhanced by the humane and chivalrous manner in which he and the men of the Deutsche Afrika Korps fought the desert campaign.

The military significance of the war in the desert — as distinct from its important political and psychological implications — was that it provided a schooling in the art of mobile warfare. For most of the campaign the forces employed were relatively small; the terrain was open and virtually limitless; there were no urban areas and no civilians — nothing but the desert and the enemy. For two years the Afrika Korps panzer divisions were the key pieces in a huge chess game where the moves on both sides were largely dictated by logistics. Rommel's supply lines led across the Mediterranean, and enormous quantities of the fuel and ammunition needed by the panzers to manoeuvre and fight were sunk by British aircraft and submarines operating from Malta. When the British were driven back to the Egyptian frontier the German supply lines on land stretched back 1,000 miles. But Rommel was a master of opportunism and his troops augmented their supplies with captured material. Many of the junior panzer leaders learned their trade in North Africa, and a number of them went on to command panzer formations in Europe and Russia after Montgomery's

arrival in Africa with increased Allied resources was destroying the panzers and annihilating the panzergrenadiers.

The special problems of the desert — the unusual strain imposed on men and machines by the sand and climate, the ever-present supply problems, the irrelevance of infantry defended localities except on vital ground, the enforced self-sufficiency of armoured formations — all taught valuable lessons which were applicable not only in the declining days of the Third Reich but in the Arab-Israeli conflicts thirty years later.

Heinz Schmidt of the 21st Panzer Division describes the panzer tactics in North Africa at the beginning of 1942, and explains why they succeeded particularly against inexperienced opponents:

'We had our first skirmish with British tanks on the second day of the march (22 January)...We sighted about thirty tanks stationary at the foot of a rise in hilly ground. When we received the order to attack, we were certain we had not been observed. We brought our 50mm anti-tank guns into position in a hollow. The enemy was totally surprised when we opened fire, and a dozen panzers raced down against the tanks. He decided his position was untenable and pulled out hurriedly with the loss of a few tanks.

Below: PzKpfw III.

Above: Panzer reinforcements for the Deutsche Afrika Korps being off-loaded at Tripoli.

We had now developed a new method of attack. With our twelve anti-tank guns we leap-frogged from one vantage point to another, while our panzers, stationary and hull-down, if possible, provided protective fire. Then we would establish ourselves to give them protective fire while they swept on again. The tactics worked well and, despite the liveliness of the fire, the enemy's tanks were not able to hold up our advance. He steadily sustained losses and had to give ground constantly. We could not help feeling that we were not then up against the tough and experienced opponents who had harried us so hard only a few weeks before . . .'

Between 28 May and 13 June 1942 Rommel attacked the British Gazala-Bir Hacheim Line, hoping to envelop the British desert flank and roll up the position. His panzer divisions circling to the south turned north inside the British positions. The British line held but behind it German and British tanks battled repeatedly around a desert crossroad called Knightsbridge.

On 28 May during the first phase of the battle Lieut Col G. P. B. Robert's 3rd Battalion Royal Tank Regiment, equipped with Grants—part of the 4th Armoured Brigade and 7th Armoured Division—were engaged south-west of El Adem. Roberts has described the action:
'We continue to move forward slowly, closing up on the light squadron and looking for a suitable hull-down position. "Gosh! There they are — more than 100. Yes, 20 in the first line, and there are six, no, eight lines, and more behind that in

the distance; a whole ruddy panzer division is quite obviously in front of us. Damn it. This was not the plan at all — where the hell are the rest of the Brigade?" However, no indecsion is possible because no alternatives present themselves.

"Hullo, Battalion Order: B and C Squadron right, C Squadron left. A Squadron (Honeys) protect the right flank from an out-flanking movement and try to get in on the enemy's flank — leave one troop on the left to keep in touch with 8th Hussars who should be coming up on our left at any moment."

The Grant squadrons were instructed to hold their fire until the German tanks were within 1,200 yards or had halted. Meanwhile our gunners, the famous Chestnut troop, had heard the situation on the wireless and were going into action behind us . . .

The leading enemy tanks had halted about 1,300 yards away; all our tanks were firing, there was no scarcity of targets, certainly two of our tanks were knocked out, but the enemy had also had losses. I could see one tank burning, and another slewed round and the crew "baling out" . . .

"Peter (my adjutant), tell Brigade we are holding our own but I do not anticipate being able to stay here for ever" . . . Our instructions were to hold on as long as possible . . .

Further tank casualties had been inflicted on both sides, but as far as the Germans were concerned as soon as one tank was knocked out another took his place; they merely use their rear lines of tanks to replace casualties in the front line and attempted no manoeuvre. On the

other hand, from well in their rear a few tanks and some anti-tank guns were being moved very wide round our right flank and the light squadron was getting more and more strung out keeping them under observation.

"Peter, tell Brigade we cannot hang on here much longer, either there will be nothing left, or we will be cut off, or both."

"Driver, advance slightly into line with the other tanks."

"75 gunner, enemy tank straight ahead receiving no attention — engage."

Hullo! there is a dashing German on the left, he has come right forward against C Squadron who have withdrawn a little, just the job for the 37mm.

"37 gunner traverse left, traverse left, traverse left — on; enemy tank broadside — 500 — fire. 37 gunner — good — have a couple more shots and then get ready with the co-ax. . . ."

War in Tunisia was, according to one Rifle Brigade officer, 'a gentleman's affair. Everybody packed up when the sun went down'. Between February 14 — 22 in a desperate battle for the Kasserine Pass, Rommel's panzers launched a surprise attack on the US II Corps positions. The American 1st Division was cut to pieces and the German advance continued in the best blitzkrieg style with the Luftwaffe bombing and strafing ahead of the panzers. To stop the drive the 26th Armoured Brigade of the British 6th Armoured Division was rushed up, and a series of actions were fought with the Allies trying to prevent the panzers from infiltrating round the flanks of the

Americans holding the Pass. Lieut Colonel Gore, commanding the 10th Bn of The Rifle Brigade, describes one of the actions:

'As it grew dark on the evening of 21 February a squadron of the Lothians* and the 17th/21st Lancers, after a day of fierce, uneven fighting, came into harbour near the Battalion. Suddenly some tanks following behind them opened fire on 'B' and 'C' Companies. They were enemy who had passed through the Leicestershire Regiment, led, according to one story, by a captured Valentine, and motored into the harbour close on the heels of Brigade . . . One of these tanks, passing near a rifleman of 12 Platoon who was digging a slit trench, was invited by the digger "to keep away from my ——— trench, you're knocking it in", a remark which sent a revolver bullet whistling past his ear. Confusion in the harbour was extreme. The Germans shouted in good English "Hands up — come out; surrender to the panzers". It was almost impossible to distinguish which were our tanks in the dark until a gunner scored a direct hit on the German tank so that it went up in flames. By the light of this fire nine German tanks were soon ablaze and their daring attempt was thwarted. No German motor infantry were in evidence, although for the rest of the night alarms were many and firing profuse.'

Five French Moroccans were the first Allied troops to clash with a 'Tiger' in North Africa. The action took place in

*The Lothian and Border Light Horse.

Above: PzKpfw VI in Tunisia. The war in the desert was used by both sides as a testing ground in the continuing guns versus armour race. Among other developments it saw the introduction of the long 75mm L/48 gun on the PzKpfw IV Ausf.G, the Tiger, the Grant/Lee series of American tanks and, of course, the Sherman

Tunisia and the French watched stunned as their 75mm shells ricocheted off the armour of the giant Tigers at a range of 50 yards.

The DAK had less than thirty Tigers in Africa at the time but some of them were used very effectively against the Americans in the Faid Pass and against the British during Operation Oxhead. (A lone Tiger was the first to break into the Sidi Nsr defences repulsing six-pounder anti-tank fire and destroying two of the enemy vehicles.)

Many of the Tigers suffered from mechanical breakdowns simply because they had been released from the factories too soon. But their breakdowns did not detract from the legendary reputation they acquired in the field. On 18 October 1943 a lone Tiger was responsible for destroying 18 Russian tanks. It was an extraordinary feat, establishing Sergeant Sepp Rannel as the first Tiger ace and earning him a Knight's Cross.

Rommel's panzers crashed through the Kasserine Pass on 18 February and fanned out northwards.

Heinz Schmidt was in the lead of the 10th Panzer Division's advance from Gafsa to Feriana and Kasserine. He recalls that he and his men were exhilarated at the thought of encountering Americans in battle for the first time, and their exhilaration was enhanced after a minor skirmish for an oasis when Schmidt discovered that the Americans had abandoned some trucks full of rations and cigarettes. Next day Schmidt received orders from his commanding officer, Major Meyer, to take the lead with his company of panzergrenadiers and some of the heavy

Panzerjäger tank destroyers, and advance down the road to Feriana. A few American tanks were seen on the way and there was some shelling. But it was not until they were approaching the actual village that any real opposition became apparent. When Schmidt's men came under machine gun fire, the whole battalion put into operation the battle drill for clearing villages.

Schmidt describes what happened:
'The rest of the battalion detrucked swiftly and we went in, infantry-fashion, on a broad front. The sniping stopped. Out of the houses poured a number of Arabs — men, women and children, waving and shouting in the false jubilation which these people always accorded any apparently victorious troops. Their sheikh recognized me as the officer in command and ran to me with outstretched arms. He gibbered words of greeting. But my right hand was on my automatic, just in case. He fumbled at me and tried to kiss my hands. When I pulled back in disgust, he grovelled on his knees and kissed my boots.

The Arabs . . . pointed out a minefield, warned us that American artillery had only just pulled out, and said that there were still a number of heavy tanks on the far side of the village.

The minefield was newly laid, and the fresh-turned soil betrayed the presence of each mine clearly. We picked our way through gingerly, with sappers at our heels marking the track for the guns behind.

Beyond the minefield the road began to climb again. I was rounding a sharp curve when I sighted and recognized a Sherman tank on the road ahead, within attacking range. I jerked the wheel in the driver's

Left: PzKpfw III and Kettenkrad, Tunisia February 1943.

Below: PzKpfw IV.

Bottom: PzKpfw II (left), PzKpfw IV (right).

hand the vehicle swerved sharply towards the left bank of the road. The detachment manning the gun immediately behind me were swift in taking their cue. In a matter of seconds they had jumped from their seats, unlimbered, swung round and fired their first shell, while the Americans still stood immobile, the muzzle of the tank gun pointing at a hillock half-right from us. Our first shell struck the tank at an angle in the flank. The tank burst into flames.

We probed ahead and soon ran into fire from tanks and machine guns deployed on either side of the road. Sending a runner back to Major Meyer with word of the situation, I deployed my company under cover of our anti-tank guns to attack the rise on our right ... Steady fighting went on for an hour. Then thick columns of black smoke rose ahead, followed by explosions, obviously an ammunition dump. The enemy tanks ceased firing. We continued to advance ...

... We went without sleep, without food, without washing, and without conversation beyond the clipped talk of wireless procedure and orders. In permanent need of almost everything civilised, we snatched greedily at anything we could find, getting neither enjoyment nor nourishment.

The daily routine was nearly always the same — up at any time between midnight and 0400 hrs; move out of the *lager* before first light; a biscuit and a spoonful of jam or a slice of *wurst* (if one was lucky!); a long day of movement and vigil and encounter, death and fear of death until darkness put a limit to vision and purpose on both sides; the pulling in of sub-units which had been sent out on far-flung missions; the final endurance of the black, close-linked march to the *lager* area; maintenance and replenishment and more orders — which took one to midnight; and then the beginning of another 24 hours.'

The Balkans

To secure the German southern flank prior to the invasion of Russia Hitler pressured Yugoslavia's Prince Regent, Paul, into joining the Axis. (18 divisions were already stationed in Hungary and Rumania). In the meantime the British, anticipating German intervention in the Balkans, sent troops from the Middle East to Greece. Encouraged by this move, anti-German elements in Yugoslavia staged a coup d'etat, deposing Prince Paul and denouncing the Axis Alliance.

Hitler was furious, and responded by ordering his generals to mount an immediate attack against both Yugoslavia and Greece. The German planners did so in ten days — an amazing demonstration of efficient military staff work. Field Marshal Siegmund List's Twelfth Army and a special Panzer Group under General der Kavallerie Ewald von Kleist, both of which were concentrating in Hungary and Rumania preparatory to the invasion of Russia, were shifted to southwest Rumania and Bulgaria opposite the eastern Yugoslav and Greek borders. General Maximilian von Weichs's Second Army also began to assemble in Austria and Hungary, opposite northern Yugoslavia. (The Italian Second Army from Trieste, and the Hungarian Third Army were

supposed to assist too. In the event their contribution to the campaign was negligible.) Because there were few roads and virtually no railways in the mountainous Balkan terrain, the German General Staff concluded that the operation against Yugoslavia and Greece could only be brought to a speedy and successful conclusion by using mechanised formations and no less than one third of Germany's total number of tanks was deployed with the attacking formations. Meantime both the Yugoslavs and the Greeks believed that they would be safe in their mountain fortresses and that the blitzkrieg techniques so successful in Poland, France and the Low Countries would not work in the Balkans. They could not have been more wrong.

On 6 April 1941 the Germans launched their assault. Preceded by an airstrike on Belgrade which paralysed the Yugoslav High Command, *Panzertruppen* spearheaded an assault which slashed into Yugoslavia from the north-east and south-east. Most of the regular Yugoslav Army of 17 infantry and 3 cavalry divisions had been deployed to hold the mountain passes. Lacking anti-tank weapons, the Yugoslavs were no match for the Wehrmacht whose mountain divisions stormed the Yugoslav positions while the panzers drove straight on through the valleys. On the left flank of the Twelfth Army the 2nd and 9th Panzer Divisions quickly reached Skoplje, and turned south-west to link up with the Italians fighting in Abania. 2nd Panzer Division then veered south-east and

Below: Panzergrenadiers of the 8th Panzer Division on the march in the Balkan theatre of operations 1941. Their vehicles are of the early series of SdKfz 251, first known as the *Mittlerergepanzerter Mannschaftskraftwagen* and later as the *Mittlerer Schützenpanzerwagen* (SPW = Medium Armoured Personnel Carrier). These three-quarter tracked vehicles were the forerunners of the modern APC 'battle-taxi'.

Below right: PzKpfw III in Rumania, Summer 1942.

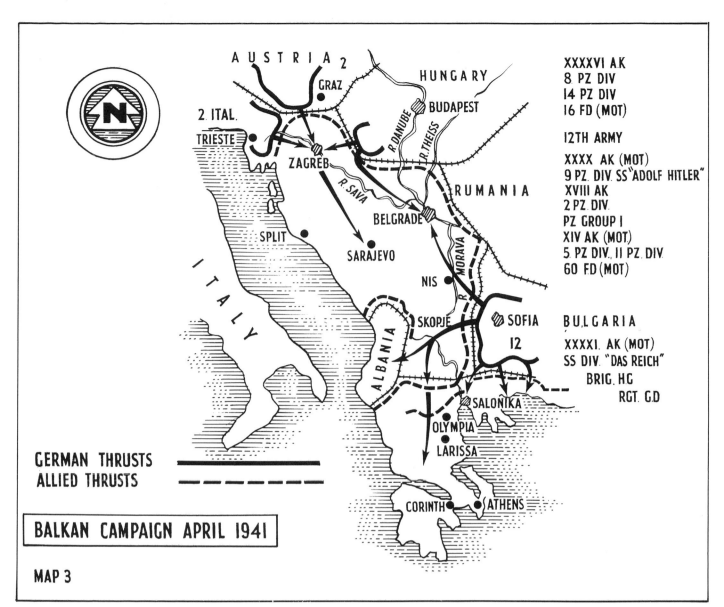

AUSTRIA 2
HUNGARY
GRAZ
BUDAPEST
2. ITAL.
R. DANUBE
R. THEISS
TRIESTE
ZAGREB
R. SAVA
RUMANIA
SPLIT
BELGRADE
SARAJEVO
R. MORAVA
NIS
SKOPJE
SOFIA
ALBANIA
12
SALONIKA
OLYMPIA
LARISSA
CORINTH
ATHENS
ITALY
BULGARIA

XXXXVI AK
8. PZ DIV
14 PZ DIV
16 FD (MOT)

12TH ARMY

XXXX AK (MOT)
9 PZ. DIV. SS "ADOLF HITLER"
XVIII AK
2 PZ. DIV.
PZ GROUP I
XIV AK (MOT)
5. PZ DIV., II PZ. DIV.
60 FD (MOT)

XXXXI. AK (MOT)
SS DIV. "DAS REICH"
BRIG. HG
RGT. G.D

GERMAN THRUSTS ——————
ALLIED THRUSTS — — — — —

BALKAN CAMPAIGN APRIL 1941

MAP 3

Above: An 'Orders Group'. Briefing before an operation besides two assault guns: Sturmgeschütz III Ausf.G (left) and *Hummel* (Bumble Bee) (right). The *Hummel* mounted a 150mm gun on a PzKpfw IV chassis. Others were built on PzIII chassis.

Top right: PzKpfw V Panther, Rumania 1944. Note the tent arrangement to accommodate the tank crew on the rail low-loader.

Bottom right: A medium armoured personnel carrier (SdKfz 251/1) fitted for patrol work in an area where partisans were operating. (In this case Yugoslavia, but similarly improvised vehicles were common in Russia). Note the V-shaped armoured ram at the front to enable the vehicle to smash through an obstacle when it ran into an ambush.

pressed down into Greece. Meanwhile on the Twelfth Army's right flank, the 5th Panzer Division and the SS-Panzer Division *Das Reich* had turned north to fight their way up the Morava River valley towards Belgrade, completely ignoring Yugoslav forces on their flanks. The Second Army was also on the move. As the 8th Panzer Division headed for Zagreb, the 14th Panzer Division and the 16th Motorized Infantry Division drove towards Belgrade. None of the armoured formations found the terrain to be impassable, but it was cetainly very difficult. The few roads in existence which became the axes of advance necessarily had to carry not only the fighting formations but their supplies, and many of them were so narrow that it was possible to operate only on a one-way system. Bad weather made the going worse. Winter snow obliterated the roads in the mountains, and icy winds did more to hold up movement than the enemy.

Despite these handicaps Zagreb fell on 10 April and Belgrade two days later when the 14th Panzers motoring down from the north joined hands with the 5th Panzers approaching from the south. Sarajevo was captured on 15 April and Yugoslav resistance ended in unconditional surrender on 17 April. German losses totalled only 558, while more than 345,000 Yugoslavs became prisoners of war. More important than this measure of success, however, the panzers could now be withdrawn and all the resources of the Twelfth Army and

Kleist's panzers could be directed to the battle of Greece.

The invasion of Greece had in fact started simultaneously with the assault on Yugoslavia. If anything the mountainous terrain around the fortified 'Metaxas Line' where the Greeks had decided to stand and fight was even worse than that on the borders of Yugoslavia. However List's mountain divisions quickly penetrated the Greek defences and German spearheads reached the sea at Salonika on 9 April. Cut off, the Greek Second Army holding the Metaxas Line surrendered and Kleist's panzers moved rapidly westwards towards where the British were preparing defensive positions between Mount Olympus and Salonika. Driving south from Skoplje the 5th Panzer Division struck through the Monastir Gap held by a Greek division protecting the British left flank. The Greeks crumbled and the road to Mount Olympus was now open.

On 13 April the 2nd Panzer Division was ordered to bypass Mt. Olympus while the Wehrmacht's 6th Mountain Division attacked it frontally. In the event the terrain here did prove to be all but impassable and even the pack animals of the *Gebirgsjäger* had difficulty negotiating the lower slopes of the famous mountain. Nevertheless some of the 2nd Division's panzergrenadiers did manage to slip round the British positions during the night, and were followed by oxen and donkeys carrying ammunition and supplies. Fearing that they would be

encircled and isolated, the British abandoned Mount Olympus and withdrew to new positions at famed Thermopylae. From then it was only a matter of a week and the campaign was over.

The Greeks capitulated on 23 April and the British abandoned Thermopylae the next day, pulling back into the Peloponnese where they were subsequently evacuated by the Royal Navy. A German airborne drop at Corinth on 26 April almost closed th withdrawal route, and before the evacuation was completed the panzers had smashed their way to the coast and were shooting up the British transports.

Success could be attributed to the bold use of panzers over supposedly impassable terrain. The operations in both Yugoslavia and Greece were models of precision and efficiency, with the *Panzertruppen* systematically carving up the opposition and annihilating it piecemeal. Once again a claim that a region was 'untankable' was disproved. Except for the area round Mount Olympus the panzers had shown that they could negotiate difficult country even when climatic conditions were unfavourable. But there was a price to pay. The wear and tear on the vehicles necessitated almost every vehicle going off the road for three weeks of overhaul. This was the main lesson of the Balkan campaign — a lesson which was to be repeated time and again in Russia.

Right: Panzer General Hans Cramer. Commanded the 8th Panzer Regiment at the start of the war. Subsequently became the commander of the OHK mobile task force.

Far right: Panzer General Gustav Fehn, who commanded the 5th Pz Div and subsequently the XXXth Pz Corps, and XXIVth Pz Corps. He was killed by Jugoslav partisans in June 1945.

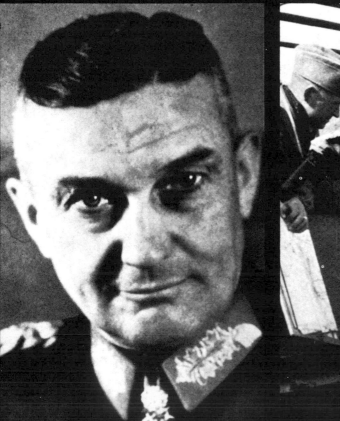

Far left: Panzer General Walter Model. Commanded the 3rd Panzer Division, succeeded General Reinhardt as commander of the XXXXlst Pz Corps; subsequently commanded the 9th Army, Army Group North, Northern Ukraine and Army Group B. Holder of the highest decoration for bravery: the Iron Cross with diamonds.

Left: German generals whose names are not familiar to English and American audiences were Panzer General Hans Hube (seen here, centre, in the armoured command vehicle) and General Count von Richthofen, whose VIIIth Flying Corps provided the panzers with close support. (Richthofen with field-glasses.) Hube, who was killed in April 1944, commanded the 16th Pz Div and then the 1st Pz Army.

Left: A notable feature of panzer operations was reliance on verbal orders — even in the higher echelons. Guderian is seen here briefing Lieut General Model after the encirclement of Kiev.

Below left: General Ludwig Crüwell was one of the panzer commanders who earned his laurels with Rommel. When he was captured by the 8th Army in North Africa in 1942 Crüwell was commanding the 11th Panzer Division.

Above: Panzer General Walther Nehring commanded the 18th Pz Div, and subsequently the XXIV Pz Corps and the 1st Pz Army.

Left: General Wilhelm von Thoma, the commander of the 20th Pz Div is seen here in North Africa in 1942 with his captor — General (later FM) Montgomery. Montgomery was criticised for shaking the hand of an enemy when the photograph was published.

Right: General Hermann Hoth, another panzer expert, is one of the most underestimated of the German generals. Seen here with Rommel, 'Papa' Hoth was commanding an infantry corps when war broke out. In France and Russia Hoth commanded a panzer group and between them he and Guderian encircled half a million Russians at Smolensk. But, like many professional soldiers, Hoth clashed with Hitler and in December 1943 was dismissed, spending the rest of the war in retirement.

Far left: Rommel, shortly after his arrival in North Africa, seen with the Italian commander-in-chief, General Gariboldi.

Left: Field Marshall Baron von Kleist was a cavalryman who commanded the XXII Panzer Corps in Poland in 1939 and a Panzer Group in France in 1940. (The latter comprised Guderian's XIX Corps and Reinhardt's XLI — five tank divisions and three of motorised infantry.) If there had been an invasion of England it would have been von Kleist's tanks which would have been put ashore on the south coast and directed towards Bristol.

Top left: General Heinz Wilhelm Guderian, the creator of the *Panzertruppe*. To the German people he was, in his heyday, a hero — and his soldiers worshipped him./*Podzun Verlag*

Bottom left: General Erich Hoepner (above, sitting) was another of Germany's best panzer generals, thought by some to be even better than Guderian and Hoth. In the early part of the Russian campaign Hoepner commanded the 4th Panzer Army under Field Marshal von Leeb (below, sitting at desk). Hoepner was opposed to Nazism and as his ideas did not agree with those of von Leeb his outspokenness led to his being dismissed by Hitler. Subsequently Hoepner was executed for his involvement in the Stauffenberg plot to kill Hitler./*Podzun Verlag*

Below: General Paul Hausser was the most able of the SS military commanders. (Guderian called him 'one of the most outstanding wartime leaders'.) In the great tank battle at Kursk, Hausser successfully commanded the SS Panzer Corps in Hoth's 4th Panzer Army. In 1943 Hitler ordered him to defend Kharkov at all costs; Hausser disobeyed and withdrew — incurring Hitler's wrath but thereby saving two vital panzer divisions and the *Grossdeutschland* Panzergrenadiers from certain destruction. Subsequently Hausser, as commander of the 7th Army, organised the successful withdrawal of the German troops in the Falaise Gap and, after von Kluge's death, commanded Army Group B./*Podzun Verlag*

Russia 1941-1943

Below: Panzergrenadiers of Guderian's Group (note the 'G' on the APCs) in the central sector June 1941 . . .

Far right: . . . . and others of the 2nd Pz Division.

The Balkan campaign upset the time-table for the invasion of Russia, but Hitler refused to be deflected from what he considered was the final step essential to the fulfilment of his *Lebensraum* dreams. The invading army was assembled in the third week of June. Close on three million men, 3,000 tanks, thousands more first and second line vehicles, artillery and all the other impedimenta essential to a huge attacking force were concentrated in the forests and woodlands near the Russian border in Poland. The fact that every man of the invading force was in position at dawn on Sunday, 22 June illustrates the mobility and flexibility of the Wehrmacht in 1941 and the perfection of its administration, since getting them there was not merely a matter of loading troops into trucks, driving them a given number of miles and telling them to get out. The move had to be made at night,

without the aid of headlamps; the men had to debus in total darkness and almost total silence; while the panzers and artillery — operating under the same conditions — had to move into position with the least possible noise. And all — men, panzers, guns and supplies — had to be kept out of sight of Russian frontier watch-towers by dawn. Then, throughout the daylight hours the men had to be fed and somehow kept interested. They had not been told what was intended by their superiors.

Among the waiting troops theorising was rife. For example besides being loaded with fuel, each panzer had ten cans of petrol secured to its turret, and it dragged behind it a trailer containing three barrels, each holding forty-five gallons more. For some this settled the question of the forthcoming operation. They argued that a bullet through a can of petrol would set a tank ablaze, and one

through a barrel would transform both tank and trailer into an incendiary bomb. So they were not being sent into battle; probably, by agreement with Stalin, they were to march through southern Russia and the Caucasus into Persia to run the British out of the Middle East and secure the oil there for Germany.

At 10pm on the Saturday (21 June) the waiting came to an end and the theorising was settled. The Panzers were ordered to move up to their respective start lines and in the gloom the tank commanders read an order from the Führer; they were to march against Russia.

Preceded by the customary aerial bombardment the onslaught started at 3am, simultaneously along a 3,250km front. Including the Finnish Army in the far north and Italian, Hungarian and Slovak units on the southern flank, 150 Axis divisions (130 of them German) were deployed in the initial phase. There were 19 panzer divisions, 10 motorised infantry divisions, 4 motorised SS divisions, the motorised *Gross-deutschland* Regiment and some independent assault-gun units. The German estimate of the Russian forces

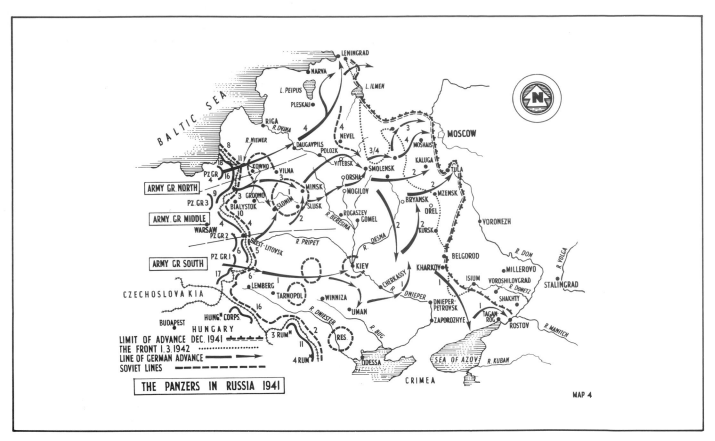

THE PANZERS IN RUSSIA 1941

MAP 4

deployed against them was 180 divisions supported by 10,000 tanks. But the latter were dispersed among the Soviet infantry divisions, and in experience and training the German troops were certainly superior to the Russians. On the other hand the limitless expanse of Russia, its harsh winter and unusual weather conditions were considered to be compensatory factors so far as the Soviet troops were concerned. And this proved to be true. In 1941 the mobility of striking power of the panzer formations led almost automatically to German victories. But the distances which had to be covered limited their tactics, as well as causing breakdowns and supply problems, and the crisis at the end of the 1941 can be attributed almost certainly to the vastness of Russia and its climate.

The Course of the Operations

The invasion plan may be summarised as follows:

(1) Field Marshal von Rundstedt's Army Group South, consisting of four armies (including one Rumanian) and General Paul von Kleist's First Panzer Group was to advance towards Kiev and the Dnieper Valley, enveloping and destroying all Russian forces between the Pripet Marshes and the Black Sea.

(2) Field Marshal Fedor von Bock's Army Group Centre, of two armies and two panzer groups Guderian's Second, and General Hermann Hoth's Third Panzer Group, would follow the traditional invasion route: Warsaw — Smolensk — Moscow. Its armoured pincers were to meet on the upper Dnieper, then capture Moscow.

(3) Meanwhile General Wilhelm von Leeb's Army Group North, of two armies and General Erich Hoepner's Fourth Panzer Group, would advance north-east towards Leningrad, pinching the Leningrad zone against the Baltic Sea. In support of these operations the Finnish Army was to occupy the Karelian Isthmus, so threatening Leningrad from the north. And still further north General Nikolaus von Falkenhorst's army in Norway was to cut the Russians' Murmansk — Leningrad supply line.

The German High Command were confident that the plan would work; they considered that the Russian military machine would collapse in eight to ten weeks and its demise would be followed by that of the Soviet political regime. Indeed they were so confident that they had made no preparations for equipping the Wehrmacht with the winter clothing which would be necessary if the operation did not go according to plan*

The First Panzer Group in the South

Von Rundstedt's Army Group was divided into two parts. On the southernmost section of this front the Eleventh Army, together with the Rumanian Army, remained in Rumania to safeguard the Rumanian oil. They did not begin to advance towards the Black Sea until 1 July.

In the northern section the terrain made the going difficult. The weather in eastern Europe had been abnormal since the spring, and the usual floods of May — when the snow melts — had been more widespread than was customary, and they had not subsided by the middle of June as they usually did. Intermittent rains added to the sogginess and turned the roads into quagmires. Within a few days of the start of the advance von Kleist's panzers were having a rich foretaste of the Russian autumn mud — the *rasputitza*.

The roads were probably worse here than in any other part of Russia, and they were incredibly bad elsewhere. Also there were very few of them, and of railways there were fewer still. An area of some

* The Luftwaffe and the Waffen-SS were not so neglectful.

Far left, centre: Central Front Russia, Summer 1941. In the headlong rush of the advance more tanks were put out of action by the terrain than by the Russians. Here a PzKpfw IV of the 7th Panzer Division is being recovered from a stream which it failed to cross. Note the reserve of petrol cans on the back of both the disabled tank and that which is pulling it out. The bridge crossed by the *Schützenpanzer* was probably erected by one of the specially trained armoured engineer battalions assigned to the panzer divisions.

Far left, bottom: The appearance of the Soviet T-34 tank undoubtedly came as a great surprise to the German panzer crews. Until well into 1943 the T-34 was 'the best tank in the world' — according to General Guderian, and the Russians continued to build T-34s until 1964. According to one of the stories told about them some T-34s were driven straight from the assembly lines to the front — by women who made up a large part of the labour force in Soviet factories. Even towards the end of the war when the T-34 had lost its superiority in the field to more up-to-date German tanks the numbers thrown into battle often made the difference between defeat and victory. The illustration is in fact quite unique. It was taken soon after a German assault gun had rammed a T-34. Both vehicles were damaged and some of the gun crew were injured. (Two of them with bandaged heads are seen with other German troops.) The hatch of the Russian vehicle was jammed but the Germans opened it with a crowbar and one of the wretched Russians inside is being pulled out by his collar. It is a picture of fear, humanity and war!

Above left: 'Command' tanks of von Kleist's Panzer Group I somewhere in the Ukraine 19 August 1941.

Right: Panzergrenadiers advancing through a Ukrainian cornfield.

Below: Sturmgeschütz III with the short 75mm L/24 gun. The 'G' on the vehicles indicates they are units of the Guderian Group. The photograph was taken in the autumn of 1941, when the Germans were harassed by time, space and 'General Mud'.

50,000 square kilometres, from Brest-Litovsk to Gomel to Colm to Kiev, from Baranowicze to Rovno was served only by three lines, and this was typical. The terrain, the natural obstacles of small rivers, marshes and large tracts of forest all regulated the tempo of the advance and this had not been allowed for in the time-table.

Kleist's First Panzer Group was expected to forge ahead, penetrate deeply into Russian territory at speed, and with the aid of the Sixth, Seventh and Eleventh Armies carry out a vast encircling movement. But von Kleist's panzers were soon in difficulties, for the Russians had expected the Germans to attack in the south and had concentrated most of their armour in this region. In consequence apart from the problems associated with the terrain, and blown bridges and heavy fighting, von Kleist's units encountered Russian T-34 tanks in large numbers, and with numbers of other equally formidable Russian colossi, the KVI and KV2.* When the panzers met the KVs they were more taken aback than they had been by the T-34 although it was the latter that impressed them most. But for the fact that the Russian tank units were not organised properly and Russian tank tactics weak, their superiority in numbers on this front — 2,000 tanks to 600 German panzers — would almost certainly have prevented the Germans from crossing the Dniester.

* These monsters, named after Marshal Kliment Voroshilov, weighed 43 tons and were 17 tons heavier than the T-34, and the T-34 with its 76.2mm gun was superior in armour and armament to the most powerful German tank of that time, the PzKpfw IV.

As it was when General Hube, commanding 16 Panzer Division in the First Panzer Group, declared that 'The advance goes forward slowly but surely', he was voicing the exact reverse of what the German High Command had intended. By 2 July, the tenth day of the fighting, von Kleist's panzers had advanced only about 100km and no breakthrough had been achieved.

Then von Kleist's luck appeared to change. On 7 July his advance guard occupied Berdichev and a few days later 13 Panzer Divison was fighting on the outskirts of Kiev. But they were unable to get any further until 16 September, when Guderian's panzers from the north sliced around the eastern edges of the Pripet Marshes to meet Kleist's Group near Lokhvitsa. It was the greatest encirclement movement in modern military history. With five Russian armies trapped inside the great bend of the Dnieper the Germans now began to tighten the ring. The city of Kiev itself was captured on 18 September and the crossing of the Dnieper followed. The Russians did not make any effective attempt to break out, although their commander Marshal Budenny did order his men to fight to the last man. In the event 665,000 Russians marched into captivity on 26 September.

The First Panzer Group now became the 1st Panzer Army. Reinforced by the Italian Expeditionary Force, one Rumanian Army and one mechanized Slovakian division, the panzers resumed the advance eastwards. On 15 October they arrived at the Don and were threatening Rostov which fell on 20 November. By this time however the German supply system was strained to the breaking point by the immense

Below: Winter 1943. PzKpfw IV (rear) and PzKpfw VI Tiger I on the central sector of the Russian front.

distances, and all the vehicles were showing the strain of terrific pace and long marches.

Only two days after occupying Rostov a Russian counter attack drove the panzers out of the city and they were compelled to retire to positions at Mius some 60km west of Rostov. There they remained, fighting numerous defensive battles until the summer of 1942.

With the Second and Third Panzer Group on the Central Front

The assault on the central sector got off to a good start. Five minutes before H-hour a section of 3 Panzer Division seized the Kodener Bridge over the Bug near Brest-Litovsk, and units of 17 Panzer Division captured the road and rail bridges on the southern side of the city. Further north, where 18 Panzer Division was to cross the Bug, there were no bridges. But here some of the preparations for the invasion of England, the abandoned Operation Sea-Lion, proved not to have been wasted. The tanks in the advance guard of 18 Panzer Division had been specially water-proofed and fitted with a Schnorkel breathing, device enabling them to move through 4 metres of water. While they were swimming across the river infantrymen were also crossing in assault-craft, and by the time the last of the 80 panzers was on dry land on the far side, engineers were building a bridge. However 18 Panzer Division did not wait to see it completed; their next objective was the bridge over the Lesna which had to be captured intact if the advance of XLVII Panzer Corps was not to be held up.

On this division's left flank 17 Panzer Division was making for Slonim, 160km north-north-east of Brest-Litovsk while the remaining formations of XLVII Panzer Corps — the 29th Motorised Infantry Division was heading north towards Bialystock. The two panzer divisions cut their way through Russian held territory with the ease of a wire slipping through cheese, but the advance of the motorised infantry division was slowed by strong Russian forces south-east of Bialystock.

Anticipating that it might be necessary to send some of 17 Panzer Division to help 29 Motorised Division, Guderian set out for the panzer division's headquarters at Slonim about 8.30am on the morning of 24 June. (The panzer generals, unlike their counterparts in the infantry, always made a point of being close to where their troops were meeting the greatest resistance). Fifteen miles outside Slonim he suddenly found himself in the middle of a battle between dismounted motor-cycle troops of 17 Panzer Division and some Russian infantry. Putting himself behind a machine gun in his armoured command truck, Guderian joined in. But it was half an hour before he was able to get through to his destination. There on the western outskirts of Slonim, he and General von Arnim, the 17th Panzer Division commander, had a narrow escape when two Russian tanks on a suicide mission attempted to shoot their way into the headquarters.

After this diversion, Guderian demanded to visit the headquarters of 18 Panzer Division. Saying that he would

Below: Ski troops worked with panzers mainly in anti-partisan operations. Officers' dress hardly differed from that of the troops; the 'Russian Cap' worn by Panzergrenadiers and some panzer crews did not carry insignia of rank. Away from their vehicles German troops were barely distinguishable from Russian troops — except by their weapons.

return to Slonim by the middle of the afternoon he commandeered a tank to take him across country to the 18th Division's HQ near Lasna. Having satisfied himself that the Division had no particular problems he issued orders for it to push on the Baranovicze, some 30km north-east of Lasna. At the same time he radioed 29 Motorised Division, instructing it to move up to Slonim as quickly as possible.

By 3.30pm he was back in Slonim, and after a short break embarked in his armoured command truck to return to his Group HQ. The day had been full of surprises — not unwelcome to a general of Guderian's audacity — and there were more to come. Only a few miles out of Slonim, unknown to the Germans, a battalion of Soviet infantry had been brought up in lorries and the Russian troops had just started to debus when Guderian arrived. Realising that if he had turned round the Russians would know they had a stranger in their midst Guderian ordered his driver to put his foot down and drive on. The Russians were slow to react and before anything could be done to detain it Guderian's vehicle was out of sight.

Back at his Group HQ Guderian learned that the XII Army Corps had made contact with the XXIV Panzer Corps on its right and XLVII Panzer Corps on its left. But the flank of 17 Panzer Division was seriously threatened by the Russians retreating from Bialystok and to protect it he gave orders for the 29th Motorised Infantry Division to engage the retreating Russians. Similar orders were sent to General Lemelsen's XLVII Panzer Corps which had been in reserve until the bridges across the Bug were cleared, and which had been advancing slowly behind the left wing of the Panzer Group.

(This reserve Corps consisted of the 10th Panzer Division, the famous SS-Panzer Division *Das Reich* and the equally famous *Grossdeutschland* Regiment which had not yet officially been expanded to divisional strength but whose strength was much greater than that of a conventional infantry regiment.)

Although he did not know it, while Guderian had been dodging Russian tanks and riflemen Hitler had been expressing doubts about the conduct of the panzer operations. Fearing that the Russians in the Bialystok pocket would be strong enough to break out, he suggested that the advance of both Guderian's and Hoth's panzer groups should be halted until they had polished off the Russians in the pocket. For once and for some unknown reason, however, the German High Command flatly refused to agree with the Führer, and insisted that nothing should be done to prevent the panzers from continuing what had been, so far, highly successful operations, and that they should be allowed to sweep on to capture Minsk — the agreed first main objective after crossing the Bug. According to Guderian's time-table the panzers were scheduled to occupy Minsk in the first week of July.

This brief description of the day's activities and experiences of the

Below: Snow is cleared from around a PzKpfw III. Feldwebel Sperlovski, Panzergrenadier recalls: '. . . Soldiers shovelled snow and streamed with sweat. I have never met anyone better able to stand punishment, whether from cold or heat or anything else, than the Germans.'

commander of a panzer group illustrates the kind of warfare being waged by the Germans in the Soviet Union. There were many dangers inherent in it but reliance was placed on sheer weight of numbers to produce and maintain the essential momentum of the leading formations. Reliance was also placed on the rapid follow-up of the infantry divisions, and the confusion created among the Russians. It was a method of attack which had considerable psychological factors to bolster it. The morale of an attacking army is almost always higher than that of an army on the defensive. The psychological effect of the rapid advance of the panzers promoted the natural upsurge of morale in the attacking troops; while the effect of encirclement — necessitating a fierce struggle to break out of the enemy ring — plus the knowledge that strong enemy forces had penetrated deep into their rear, could only lead to a weakening morale among the Russian troops. The advantages, it would seem, lay entirely with the German forces. Yet the German tactics had serious limitations — deriving in the main not from the method, but from the terrain in which the method was employed. In the west, where the furthest distances from base could easily be covered by supply trains operating on extensive and competent rail and road communication systems, conditions were ideal for a blitzkrieg war. In Russia however, the situation was very different; the experts had overlooked the extremely poor railways and the almost complete absence of metalled roads. Consequently it became increasingly difficult to keep the panzers supplied with fuel. And without fuel they were stalled.

Time and again in the later days of this early period of the campaign, as the panzers penetrated deeper and deeper into Russia, officers complained of the misleading maps with which they had been supplied. What the maps showed as main roads, which the ordinary German naturally expected to be metalled, usually turned out to have a dirt surface which a shower of rain quickly converted into a quagmire where armoured vehicles bogged down.

Nevertheless, although the tempo of the advance was slowing down, the panzers in the central sector were still making spectacular progress. On 27 June the armoured pincers, whose jaws consisted of 17 Panzer Division of Guderian's Group and 7 Panzer Division of Hoth's Third Panzer Group, closed on Minsk, and four Soviet armies — almost

PzKpfw III and horse-drawn snow mobile. (Panzergunner) Oberschütze Kellermann recalls: 'The cold has remained in my memory like a frozen nightmare . . . The temperature often varied between fifteen and twenty-five below zero. I recall one horrifying day of wind when it fell to thirty-five degrees below zero, and I thought I would die. Nothing could warm us. We urinated into our numbed hands to warm them and, hopefully, to cauterise the gaping cracks in our fingers . . .'

half a million men — were trapped in the Bialystok 'pocket'. The Russians had abandoned Minsk, and had destroyed the greater part of the town before Guderian's and Hoth's men entered it. But they tried to fight their way through the German encircling line, and a fierce battle raged around Bialystok until 2 July when the Russians surrendered. Approximately 290,000 Russians were taken prisoner (the remainder being killed or wounded) and the advance to the next objective, Smolensk, could now be resumed.

During the next few days the panzer and motorised divisions pressed on towards the east. But the going became harder as the Russians improved their delaying tactics. Fortunately for the Germans many bridges across rivers were captured intact because Russian officers failed to act on their own initiative, or feared to do so. Nevertheless capturing bridges invariably entailed stiff fighting. By 10 June, however, Guderian's panzers were advancing across the Dnieper and towards Smolensk. On their left Hoth's Third Panzer Group was also making for Smolensk from the north-west.

The plan was to encircle the city with Hoth's forces and with Guderian's 17th and 18th Panzer and 20th Motorised Divisions. To frustrate this Marshal Timoshenko, who had received orders from Stalin that Smolensk was to be held to 'the last man and last round', had deployed the Soviet Sixteenth Army

across the approaches to the city. In the event, neither Timoshenko nor the Sixteenth Army could prevent Smolnesk being captured by the Germans. Although Timoshenko's troops fought with what was described by one of the panzer commanders as 'savage determination', they lacked ammunition, air support and supplies and Guderian's troops entered Smolensk on 15 July — although this did not signify the end of the fighting. Over 100,000 Soviet troops were trapped in 'pockets' around the city, and as soon as 10 Panzer Division and the *SS-Das Reich* Division arrived, Guderian set about liquidating these Russian pockets. In the course of the operations which followed there developed some of the stiffest fighting of the campaign to date. For the first time since the start of Operation Barbarossa the panzers began to feel the effect of shortages of fuel and ammunition, and this was naturally reflected in their fighting capability.

By the end of July however the isolated Russian groups had been overwhelmed, Russian counter-attacks were slackening, and Guderian was re-grouping his panzers for a further advance towards Moscow. At this stage Hitler intervened, and imposed a change in plan which was to have far-reaching consequences. At a conference at von Bock's Army Group HQ on 3 August the Führer said that he had not yet decided which of the three objectives he had in mind — Leningrad,

Moscow and the Ukraine — he should set first. Leningrad, he thought, was probably the most important. After Leningrad he tended to favour the Ukraine because the rich agricultural produce and raw materials which would fall to Germany with its capture were essential to Germany's future operations. As far as Guderian was concerned Moscow should be the next objective. But whether his panzers were going there, or were destined to take part in operations elsewhere, their worn-out tanks would have to be replaced.

While considering this request Hitler revealed that all tank replacements were having to come from current-production, and, demands for replacements could not be met as all new tanks had to be kept back for the new panzer and panzer-grenadier divisions, which were being created. (He did eventually agree, however, that 300 tank engines should be suppled to units on the Eastern Front. A figure which Guderian described as 'totally inadequate'.)

No clear orders for future action were given at this conference and three weeks were to pass before Hitler made up his mind. When he did so the effect of the directive setting out his instructions was explosive. The Ukraine was to take precedence over Moscow. And to bolster the slower-moving armies on both the Northern and Southern Fronts the Führer detached both the Second and Third

Top left: PzKpfw IV drives through a village in the Ukraine during the thrust to the Caucasus. This photograph illustrates the types of road over which reinforcements had to pass.

Bottom left: Sturmgeschütz III with 75mm L/24 gun. Neither Russians nor Germans had much concern for civilians — except as working 'units'. Some fought and died for Mother Russia. Others — including many thousands of Ukrainians — served the German conquerors as *Hivis* (abbreviation of *Hilfswillige* or voluntary helpers.) A panzergrenadier officer of the *Grossdeutschland* Division recalls: 'And I remember Russian girls, shaking with laughter when they had every reason to hate us . . . they made more noise than the men! In Kiev — a beautiful city full of flowers — in spring 1943 the streets were full of German troops walking with Ukrainian girls . . .'

Below: Not all the panzer units could be withdrawn during the winter of 1941/42. The *Geschnautz* (slang for Assault Gun) is one that remained in the Leningrad area.

Panzer Groups from von Bock's Army Group Centre. Guderian's Second Panzer Group was to go to the assistance of von Rundstedt's Army Group South, while Hoth's Third Panzer Group joined von Leeb's Army Group North. The immediate results of this unexpected change in plan were favourable. But the generals were all agreed that in the long run the new plan could only lead to the very thing they had all hoped to avoid — a winter campaign.

Protests to Hitler were unavailing and it was not until October that the attack on Moscow was resumed. Then at the beginning of winter, although the Germans made some progress, they failed to capture the Soviet capital.

Far left, top: Nor was the re-equipment of panzer divisions with PzKpfw IIIs and PzKpfw IVs completed before the 1942 offensive. This photograph of a PzKpfw 38(t) was taken near Sebastopol in June 1942.

Bottom left: Marder II 75mm *Panzerjäger* in a Russian village on the Central Front in 1942. Like the British and the Americans, the Germans often gave their vehicles names. This one *Kohlenklau* (Coal Thief) is called after a contemporary Berlin cabaret character — a cheerful spiv who made the most of fuel rationing.

Above left: The interior of a Sturmgeschütz. Note that the engine was separated from the fighting compartment by a partition; note also the rack of hand grenades for use in Soviet 'human wave' assaults.

The Fourth Panzer Group's Operations in the North

It will be recalled that the mission of von Leeb's Army Group North and Hoepner's Fourth Panzer Group was to destroy the Russian forces in the Baltic region and to occupy the Russian ports on the Baltic Sea; of these the most important was Leningrad.

The first objective and the first bound was a big road viaduct over the River Dubyssa, fifty miles inside Russian territory. No-one knew better than von Manstein who had fought in the area during World War I, that the seizure intact of this bridge was essential to the whole operation on the northern front. For most of its length the Dubyssa runs through a deep gorge whose sides are unscalable, and if the Russians destroyed the viaduct the panzers would be in a very difficult situation since no tank could negotiate the ravine. The Germans might be able to replace it, but not before the Soviet troops could organize a stubborn defence. Its capture therefore could mean the difference between success and failure.

8 Panzer Division was allotted the task, and von Manstein attached himself to them for the operation. His presence, he knew, would be a constant reminder to his subordinate commanders of the importance and urgency of the operation. And so it did, for although there was some fierce fighting in the early stages of the advance the panzers forced a gap in the Russian defences and its advance guard units raced for the Dubyssa. On their way they encountered virtually no resistance and if there had been any guards on the viaduct they had fled. The leading tanks advanced on to the bridge, ambled across to the other side and fanned out. Only then did they come under fire, and as it was only from small arms their armour was adequate protection. Hard on the tanks of the advance guard, the main body of 8 Panzer Division had been pushing their way since the breakthrough. By dusk its tanks had joined the bridgehead and 3 Motorised Division had come up to protect the southern flank.

The first indispensable objective on the road to Leningrad had fallen to the panzers without much difficulty. And in the ensuing four days the advance of 8 Panzer Division and 3 Motorised Division continued at break-neck speed. (This is not to say that the two divisions were left to progress in peace. They did, in fact, encounter strong Russian forces but were able to beat their way through, inflicting comparatively heavy losses on the Russians — 70 tanks and several batteries of artillery in one day alone.) Manstein's Corps HQ kept up with the two advancing divisions, and on the morning of 26 June he was handed a message to say that the two bridges across the Dvina at Daugavpils had been captured almost completely intact. Indeed the great road bridge was completely undamaged as the panzers had literally overrun the Russian demolition squads and knocked the explosives out of their hands. At the railway bridge the Russians had been able to ignite a small charge which did some damage, but it was so slight that the bridge was soon made serviceable. This success terminated the first stage of the German plan on the northern front.

With obvious pride von Manstein has recorded in his book *Lost Victories:* 'Before the offensive started I had been asked how long we thought we should take to reach Dvinsk [Daugavpils] assuming that it was possible to do so. My answer had been that if it could not be done inside four days, we could hardly

count on capturing the crossings intact. And now, exactly four days and five hours after H-hour, we had actually completed, as the crow flies, a non-stop dash through 200 miles of enemy territory . . . '

Up to this stage success had crowned the panzers' efforts and Manstein could well be proud of their achievements. But Hitler was having doubts and his order to pause on the Dvina resulted in a setback. The delay gave the Russians time to organize themselves and they rushed every available soldier from Pskov, Minsk and even Moscow. Within 48 hours Manstein's panzers were being assailed by forces so strong that at some points the situation was extremely critical for the Germans. Some ground was lost and considerable effort was needed to regain it. But the situation had been stablised and mopping up operations — which included the capture of Riga — had been completed when Panzer Group 4 received new orders. (By this time the SS-Panzer Division *Totenkopf* had joined von Manstein's Corps as its third mobile unit, and panzers of von Reinhardt's Corps had crossed the Dvina roughly half-way between Daugavpils and Riga.) The two corps were to advance on Pskov; the next objective was Leningrad.

On 2 July von Manstein led his corps in a north-westerly direction towards what Hitler described as 'the cradle of communism'. Russian opposition grew progressively stiffer the further the advance progressed; nearing Pskov Panzer Group 4 came up against the Stalin Line.

Unlike the Maginot Line the Stalin Line was not a continuous system of highly complex fortifications. It followed the line of the pre-1939 Russian frontier from the southern end of Lake Peipus west of Pskov in the north, down to the Black Sea. Since it made use of what natural obstacles there were, the Line was in reality a series of fortified points. But there were great gaps between the obstacles and for the most part the Panzers had only to probe to find the gaps where the natural obstacles were passable to break the Line. Here in the north, however, it presented a considerable obstacle. Von Manstein's Corps found itself trying to pick a way through a great marsh, and although 8 Panzer Division found a timbered roadway leading through the swamps, it had to clear the vehicles of a Russian motorised division which had stuck there and replace a number of bridges before it could get on. Then when the division did at last get clear of the swamps it found a strong Russian force, equipped with KVI and KVII tanks, waiting for it; and these were only overrun after heavy fighting. Meantime 3 Motorised Division had got bogged down in another part of the swamps. By 7 July, when Pskov fell, von Manstein's Panzer Corps alone had lost 6,000 men and his serviceable tanks had been reduced to nearly half-strength. Moreover the remaining panzers were feeling the strain and he told General von Paulus (at that time QMG of the German High Command, later to command at Stalingrad) that the whole of Panzer Group 4 ought to be withdrawn and given a rest. The terrain was such that a rapid advance was not possible, he said. If Leningrad was to be encircled then the infantry ought to do the job, and the panzers saved for the final thrust. Paulus agreed but the High Command did not, and von Manstein was ordered to push on to Leningrad. Commenting on the subsequent fighting he wrote 'The battles around Luga proved very tough indeed . . . ' This was scarcely surprising. The Leningrad City Soviet had mobilized every man between sixteen and sixty and every woman between sixteen and fifty, and set them to work on building a triple ring of fortifications. The outer of these rings followed the course of the River Luga — and between 14 million and

Top left: PzKpfw IIIs of von Manstein's advance guard at Sebastopol Harbour 5 July 1942.

Bottom left: Sturmgeschütz III in Kharkov June 1942. Kharkov was the German supply centre during the 1942 Caucasus offensive.

Below: Tiger I. On 28 January 1944 in the so-called Cherkassy pocket near Korsun (200km SE of Kiev) six German divisions were encircled by nine Soviet Armies. The Germans promptly ordered other troops to break the steel ring around their six divisions.

20million man-days were spent on its construction, during which 620 miles of earth walls, 370 miles of anti-tank ditches, 185 miles of wooden obstacles, 5,000 timber earth and concrete bunkers, and more than 870 miles of barbed wire entanglements were erected. This was the line which the LVI Panzer Corps had to pierce.

Once through this line the going was still tough, with bad road conditions, mines and stiffening Russian resistance slowing down the panzers' advance. The heavy summer rains which fell in the final days of August and the first days of September turned the roads into rivers of mud along which mechanised and motorised formations had great difficulty in passing. Nevertheless at the beginning of September the last land-line between Leningrad and the rest of Russia was cut; Hitler's 'cradle of communism' was surrounded, and the Germans were battering at the inner ring of defences. On 8 September the first air and artillery attacks were made on the city, and units of the Sixteenth and Eighteenth German Armies had moved up to support Panzer Group 4 in what was intended to be the final phase of the offensive against Leningrad.

On 11 September 1 Panzer Division captured the Duderhofer Hills, a key position in the Russian line of defences and the towers and factories of the city

were plainly visible to the panzers concentrating for the final assault. Victory appeared to be within their grasp when Hitler ordered the attack to be called off. He had changed his mind, he said; his original intention had been to raze the city to the ground, but now he had decided 'not to fall in with the Russian attempt to prolong the struggle in the cities by street-fighting .. , *

So the troops were given orders to dig in, Panzer Group 4 was pulled out, and after its withdrawal Leningrad was declared a secondary theatre of war.

The Road to Moscow

This account of panzer operations in 1941 would not be complete without a brief review of the battle for Moscow.

It will be recalled that, despite vigorous protests from General Guderian, the panzers on the Central Front were withdrawn and sent to bolster the invaders on the northern and southern fronts. This led directly to the fall of Kiev and the surrender of some 665,000 Russian troops when Marshal Budenny's Army Group was destroyed. Hitler then declared the generals could have their way — they could attack Miscow; and on 6 September he issued 'Führer Befehl No 35' outlining the plan for the advance on the Soviet capital.

* *Hitler als Feldherr*, Halder page 41.

Three infantry armies — the Fourth, Ninth and Second, and the three Panzer Groups (now known as Panzer Armees): Hoth's Third on the left wing, Hoepner's Fourth (what was left of it when it had been withdrawn from the Leningrad area) in the centre, and Guderian's Second Panzer Army on the right, would be employed in the operation code-named *Taifun* (Typhoon). In sum this amounted to a force of 46 infantry divisions, 14 panzer divisions, 8 motorised divisions and one motorised brigade; support would be provided by two complete airfleets and protection by numerous anti-aircraft formations. It was to be an operation which contemporary German military historians have described as 'a modern Cannae — on a greater scale.'

In ordering that it should begin about the middle of September the Führer displayed a ridiculous lack of understanding of military matters. Regrouping the forces for operation *Taifun* required time, with supplies problems and guerilla activity slowing down the preparations. Moreover it was already autumn; winter would come soon and many of the panzer commanders were uneasy about the prospect for the offensive. By 30 September however all was more or less ready. Hoepner's Fourth Panzer Army had come down from the north, and Guderian's reorganised Second Army had come up from chasing

Top left: Nashorn (Hornisse) 88mm anti-tank 43/I (L/71) on a PzKpfw IV chassis. Some of the latest weapons were used in the operations SE of Kiev.

Centre left: But as the photograph shows some of the old tanks, in this case a PzKpfw 38(t), were still in service.

Bottom left: There were very few heavy anti-tank guns in the Cherkassy pocket, and the infantry had to rely on their own anti-tank weapons to stop the Russian tanks. The most primitive of these weapons was the Molotov cocktail — a bottle containing an incendiary mixture which ignited when it hit the target. The *Panzerfaust*, carried by the infantrymen marching behind the assault gun above, was one of the best infantry anti-tank weapons of the war. Although its range was short (25 to 30 metres) the number of tanks knocked out by *Panzerfausts* testified to its effectiveness.

Above: But the Tiger tank proved to be the most effective anti-tank weapon during the 1944 campaign in Russia.

PzKpfw VI Tiger Is

Right: Panzer units, once committed to battle, were driven hard. This crew of a tank of the 3rd Panzer Division were photographed resting after the bitter fighting for Rostov in July 1942./*Podzun Verlag*

Timoshenko's armies in the south. Guderian had been promised 100 new tanks for the operation, but only half of them arrived.

Guderian attacked according to plan on 30 September, but the Third and Fourth Panzer Armies were held back and did not join the offensive until two days later. The Russians were taken completely by surprise and 4 Panzer Division drove straight into the town of Orel — to find the trains running and the population going about its affairs quite normally. Through the gap which this division had opened poured the remainder of the Second Panzer Army; following them came the infantry and artillery of the Sixth Army. The encirclement of three Red armies at Briansk was beginning. Meanwhile Hoth's and Hoepner's Panzers on the West Front were having similar successes north and south of Smolensk, and six more Russian armies were also threatened with encirclement. Apprehensive of the outcome of the German operations the Soviet High Command relieved Marshal Timoshenko of his command and appointed the hitherto unknown General Zhukov in his place.

The Russians resisted the German advance with courage and tenacity, and Guderian was concerned about their new tank tactics. 'These tactics were very

worrying', he wrote in his book *Panzer Leader*. 'Our defensive weapons available at that period were only successful against the T-34s when the conditions were ususually favourable. The short-barrelled 75mm gun of the Panzer IV was only effective if the T-34 was attacked from the rear, even then a hit had to be scored on the grating above the engine to knock it out. It required very great skill to manoeuvre into a position from which such a shot was possible. The Russians attacked us frontally with infantry, while they sent their tanks, in mass formation, on our flanks'. The Russians were also reported to be using many ruses — including dogs as living booby traps.

Despite the new tactics and determined efforts to break out of the encirclements at Viasma and Briansk, the German grip was too strong. The Russian troops at Briansk surrendered on 16 October, and those at Viasma capitulated next day. By 25 October the two battles were over and the Russians had lost another 700,000 men, more than 1,000 tanks and 5,000 guns. This brought the total of losses by the Red Army in the area of the German Central Front to one and a half million men. To Western observers as well as the Germans it seemed that the Soviet military giant had clay feet and was almost defeated.

With the fall of Viasma there was

virtually nothing to stop the panzers driving straight to the heart of the Soviet capital. In Moscow itself a wave of panic rippled through the city when it was learned that the Russian Government was fleeing to Kuibishe, 500 miles to the east, and there were disturbances which had not been seen in Moscow since the Revolution and the Civil War. However, while Zhukov was marshalling every available man, woman and child over the age of fourteen and setting them to work digging anti-tank ditches and trenches round Moscow a powerful Russian ally arrived to halt the German offensive. 'During the night of October 6/7, Guderian recorded, 'the first snow of winter fell. It did not lie long, and, as usual, the roads rapidly became nothing but canals of bottomless mud along which our vehicles could advance only at snails' pace, and with great wear to the engines. We asked for winter clothing — we had already done this once before — but were informed that we would receive it in due course and were instructed not to make further unnecessary requests of this type.'

By mid-October it was clear that the *rasputitza* had set in in earnest. 'Wheeled vehicles', wrote Guderian, 'could only advance with the help of tracked vehicles. These latter, having to perform tasks for which they were not intended, rapidly wore out.' No chains were available for towing vehicles, so the Luftwaffe dropped coils of rope to the immobilised trucks. Indeed no preparations at all had been made for the winter. Supplies of 'anti-freeze' — as essential to tanks and other vehicles as warm clothing was to the men — were demanded by the panzer generals — but, like clothing, none came.

While the panzers were immobilised the German infantry struggled forward a few miles through the swamps, but it was already clear that things were going wrong for the Germans. All the troops were exhausted, many units were down to half strength, and the panzers were down to two-fifth of their tank strength; food was short, ammunition and fuel were running out, and still no winter clothing had arrived. German casualties since 22 June now totalled three quarters of a million men.

On 12 November, however, it seemed as if things were about to take a turn for the better. The thermometer made a spectacular drop, and vehicles could move again over the frozen mud. On 15 November the Third and Fourth Panzer Armies on the left wing led an all-out assault which was intended to take them to Moscow. Two days later in the south Guderian's panzers joined in. But the Russians had brought up fresh and well equipped divisions from Siberia to stop the German advance, and fierce battles raged in blizzards and temperatures which fell to 30 degrees below zero (Centigrade). Surprised by the determination of the Russians, the exhausted panzers, out of petrol and ammunition, were compelled to break off their attack within sight of Moscow and 30km from the walls of the Kremlin. On 6 December the idea of capturing Moscow had to be abandoned — temporarily it was thought then, but in reality for ever.

Rasputitza!
Some idea of the problems associated with the mud of Russia in spring and autumn, and how tired, hungry men behave in such circumstances may be gleaned from the following. Narrated by a man who served with a panzer division supply column, the events described took place in the autumn of 1942 during the retreat from the Don to Kharkov. They could well have happened in the spring of 1943, or the spring or autumn of 1944, anywhere on the Central or Northern Fronts.

'For two days the infantry had been pulling out — either on foot or loaded in trucks; soon only a small section of the *Panzergruppe* was left. The passage of vehicles and men had turned our camp into an extraordinary quagmire: thousands of trucks, tanks, tractors and men rolled and tramped for two days and two nights through terrain running with streams of mud.

We were in the middle of this syrup, trying to reorganize the material we had to abandon. The engineers were working with us, preparing to dynamite the ammunition we had heaped against the huts, over the carcasses of eight dismantled trucks. Towards noon, we organised a fireworks display which any civil authority might have envied. Carts, sleighs, and buildings were all dynamited and burned. Two heavy howitzers which the tractors hadn't been able to pull from the mire were loaded with shells of any calibre. Then we poured any explosive that came to hand into their tubes, and shut the breech as best as we could. The howitzers were split in two by the explosions, scattering showers of lethal shrapnel. We felt exhilarated, filled with the spirit of destructive delight. In the evening, the spandaus stopped a few Soviet patrols, who had undoubtedly come to see what was happening. During our last hour, we were under light artillery fire, which caused us a certain emotion. Then we left.

After the period of light artillery fire, the troops covering the *Panzergruppe* signalled several enemy penetrations into our former positions. A hasty departure order was given. We were no longer organised to hold off the Russians for any length of time. I was carrying my belongings, looking for a vehicle, when our *Feld* [sergeant-major] assigned me to a truck we had captured from the enemy which was now carrying our wounded.

"Step on the gas!" he shouted. "We're getting out!"

Every soldier in the Wehrmacht was supposed to know how to drive. I had been given some idea of how to handle military vehicles during my training in Poland, but on machines of a very different kind. However, as one never discussed orders, I jumped into the driver's seat of the Tatra. In front of me, the dashboard presented an array of dials whose needles uniformly pointed down, a few buttons, and a series of words in indecipherable characters. The engineers had just attached the heavy truck to the back of a Mark-4. We would be leaving instantly; it was essential that I get the wretched machine to start. I considered climbing out and confessing my incapacity, but repressed the idea on reflection that they might assign me to something more difficult, or even leave me behind, to get out on my own feet as best I could.

If I couldn't move, I would be captured by the Ivans — a thought which terrified me. I pawed frantically at the dashboard, and was blessed by a miracle. My eye fell on Ernst Neubach, who was clearly looking for a lift.

My friend joyfully jumped aboard.

"I was ready to hang on to the back of a tank", he said. "Thanks for the seat".

I had no time for conversation. The powerful engine of the tank to which we were attached was already roaring, and from the turret, one of the tank men signalled to me to put the truck in gear at the same time as the tank — to reduce the jolt for the wounded. I pressed down hard on the accelerator, and the engine made a series of loud bangs.

"Gently", the *Feld* shouted at me, so I let up on the pedal. The chain stretched taut, and the heavy truck took off with a brusque jolt — producing a chorus of groans and curses behind me.

That first night of the retreat was complicated by a fine rain, which required of Ernst and me the agility and balance of acrobats simply to keep our Tatra in the wake of the Mark-4. Without the tank, we would never have been able to escape from that swamp. The driver

stepped on the accelerator in fits of irritation, dragging the Tatra, which threatened to disintegrate. The tank tracks churned the ground into a heavy syrup, which the rain thinned into soup. The windscreen became completely caked with mud, and Ernst waded through the liquid ground to scrape it away with his hands.

The blacked-out headlight had been left with only a narrow strip uncovered. Within a few minutes this strip was sealed by mud, so that we had no light at all. I couldn't even see the back of the tank, although it was no more than five metres ahead of us. Our truck, more often than not at an oblique angle to the tank, was constantly being pulled back into line by the tightly stretched chain. Each time this happened, I wondered if we still had our front wheels. Behind us, the wounded had stopped moaning. Soon after daylight the driver of our panzer suddenly turned off to the right, leaving the track, which had become impassable even for a tank, and drove straight up the scrub-covered bank. Our truck, whose wheels by this time were balls of mud, was pulled forward, while its engine rattled helplessly. Then everything came to a complete halt. (This was the second stop since our departure, as we had stopped once in the night to refuel.) The poor bastards on the back of the tank jumped down among the broken branches. Their backsides had been burning all night on the hot metal over the engine, while the rest of their bodies froze in the cold rain. An exchange of shouted abuse which was nearly a fight broke out at once between an NCO in the engineers and the Panzerführer. Everyone else took advantage of this opportunity to crap and eat.

"One hour's rest!" shouted the NCO,, who had taken on himself the leadership of the group. "Make the most of it!"

"Fuck off," shouted the Panzerführer, who had no intention of being pushed around by some half-baked engineer. "We'll leave when I've had enough sleep."

"We have to get to Belgorod this morning", the NCO said in a steely voice. He undoubtedly nourished dreams of being an officer. Then, putting his hand on the Mauser which hung at his side, he added: "We'll leave when I give the order. I've got the highest rank here, and you'll obey me."

"Shoot me if you like, and drive the tank yourself. I haven't slept in two days, and you're going to leave me the hell alone".

The other flushed crimson, but said

nothing. Then he turned to us. "You two! Instead of standing there asleep on your feet, get into the truck and help the wounded. They have their needs, too."

"That's it," added the tank driver, who was clearly looking for trouble. "And, when they're finished, the Herr Sergeant will wipe their asses."

"You'll watch it, or I'll report you," snorted the sergeant. He was now white with rage.

Inside the truck the wounded had not died, despite the jolting of the journey. They were no longer making any noise, and we could see that some of their bandages were soaked with fresh blood. Fighting the exhaustion we helped them down and back as best we could — omitting only one man, who was missing both legs. They all asked us for something to drink, and in our ignorance we gave them as much water or brandy as they wanted. We certainly shouldn't have done this: two men died a short time later.

We buried them in the mud, with sticks and their helmets to mark their graves. Then Ernst and I curled up in the cab, to try to snatch a little sleep. But sleep wouldn't come, and we lay instead, with throbbing temples, talking of peace. Two hours later, it was the tank driver who gave the order to depart, as he had predicted. It was now mid-morning. The day was clear and bright, and large chunks of snow fell slowly from the trees.

It took us a while to extricate ourselves from the bank we had driven into. However, two hours later we arrived at a village whose name I can't remember, some five miles from Belogorod. It was filled with soldiers from every branch of the army. The few streets were perfectly straight, and lined with low houses; the way the roofs sat on the walls reminded me of heads with no foreheads, whose hair grows right into the eyebrows. There were swarms of soldiers, and a multitude of rolling equipment covered with mud, pushing through the shouting mob of soldiers, most of whom were looking for their regiments. The road at this point had been roughly resurfaced, and was much more negotiable.

We unhooked ourselves from the tank, and took on eight or ten of the engineers who had been riding on its back. Somewhat bewildered by this flood of soldiers, I had stopped the truck, and was looking for my company. Two MPs told me they thought it had gone on toward Kharkov, but as they weren't sure, they sent me to the redirection center which had been organised in a trailer and was staffed by three officers, who were tearing their hair. When I was finally able to catch their attention through the thousands of shouts and gesticulations besieging them, I was harshly reprimanded for straggling. They probably would have sent me to be court-martialed, if they'd had time.'

Action!

The engagement narrated in the following pages took place during the operations of Guderian's Second Panzer Group advancing on Odessa in autumn 1941. Three tanks — 'Sea Rose One', commanded by Hauptmann Georg von Konrat, 'Sea Rose Two', commanded by Fähnrich (Officer Cadet) Olle, 'Sea Rose Three' commanded by Leutnant Walter — and two armoured cars, 'Sea Rose Four' under Fähnrich Hans and 'Sea Rose Five', Fähnrich Albert, were involved.

The advance was held up by a body of retreating Russians, some of whom were occupying positions near a bridge. Van Konrat was ordered to clear the road and he decided to take the three tanks and one armoured car on an encircling move along the edge of the forest on one side of the road. When this force emerged on the Russian 'flank' the other armoured car ('Sea Rose Five') was to try to press on up the road.

'We moved rapidly out through the trees and on to the field, immediately starting to pick up speed. At first, I could see nothing because of the smoke, but then, suddenly, we were through and into the open field, in sight of the Russian guns. Jochum, my driver, yelled, "We're doing fifty-five."

"See if you can make it sixty-five," I roared back.

Two seconds later we made our first turn, shooting out to the left in an eighty-degree twist and heading full pelt for the Russian guns. They were blasting at us non-stop, but before they could line up again we were off to the right and heading at an angle for the river. Then we went left again and back towards the turn-off. The Russians must have thought we had either gone crazy or that we were trying to cut them off from their retreating forces. We made another sharp turn back towards the river and this time I jammed the lid of the turret shut — just in case one of those grenade throwers did actually hit a bull's-eye. If we had to go out, I didn't want it to be over something as measly as that.

We turned left again, fifty-five degrees, dodged towards the forest and then were off again on a right-hand tangent before the guns had a chance to aim. The Russians were going berserk. I had my telescope up and was watching them. There were two 76mm infantry guns set up right at the edge of the road, well protected from direct hits, but beautifully able to command the field themselves. On the other side of the road, among the trees, I could plainly see a lot of heavy guns. Everything else was too well covered to be visible. But those I had seen were quite enough. I could have split my sides watching their barrels turning and twisting frantically about. They were firing half blindly, sending out shell after shell in one continuous bombardment, but none even half-hopeful of aiming the right way.

Dita was having the same trouble and I could hear just one unending stream of curses issuing from the gun turret. The main object of both the Russians and ourselves had become just to fire and fire again and if you came within fifty metres — very good. We turned left again, but this time charged off backwards and away from the Russian lines, just to prevent them working out any sort of pattern. Five seconds later, we were off again to the right and back towards the river. Now the Russians even had an old Katusha [rocket launcher] doing her bit, spraying the field with lollipops. The sky was just one mass of exploding shells. I could see the infantry digging in ahead of the guns so we charged towards them this time, machine gunning and firing madly. They dropped their spades with the first burst, and went rushig back towards the road and out of sight. I was grinning like a madman. I think we all were.

We careered off again, then right, left, backwards, forwards, left right, and off again. The tank heeled about wildly, lurching off in another direction almost before it had regained balance from the last zigzag. At times I thought we had been hit or lost our crawlers [tracks] the way Jochum was throwing the poor tank around on its sides. My stomach felt turned inside out and every now and again I almost fainted from the violent and sudden jolts. I didn't dare even think about what might be happening inside my lungs. Only the excitement was keeping me conscious.

We turned again, the tank seeming to leap feet into the air. Dita had now even given up his cursing. The gun turret was lifting so much that even when he was lucky enough to find the barrel aiming in the right direction, we had turned again by the time he fired and the shells went completely wild, whizzing over the Russians' heads, into the trees, into the ground, anywhere, everywhere. We kept

it up hoping madly that each turn woudn't be the unlucky one, the time when we drove ourselves straight into a shell, and watching for Sea Rose Two, Three and Four to come charging in for a good view of the road from the forest where I felt nothing short of magic would drive them out. I was just hoping that our brand of magic would prove good enough.

The infantry were massing around again so I ordered my driver to race back in towards them again. Otherwise, they could jump on my other tanks and throw grenades down the turrets. "Right into them for a hundred metres next turn," I yelled. Jochum didn't answer. He didn't have time to. With a sharper than ever spin to the left the whole tank seemed to keel over. But it steadied itself on the brink and came up again. Now our gun turret was steady and Dita grinning. He could shoot direct contact into the Russian gun positions. Our machine guns cross-fired into the infantry, sending them flying, while Dita sent over his roughly calculated shots, distracting the guns.

We hurtled off to the right, then backwards, and right again, and off across the field. "In again!" I bellowed. We turned and charged for the infantry lines, but this time Jochum lost control of the tank completely and we found ourselves hurtling down on the infantry closer and closer, until I began to fear we'd overrun the road itself. Now we were within three hundred metres of them and still going. If the Russians weren't laughing with glee, they were shivering in their boots. I could see men flying out and leaving their guns in all directions as our tank roared down full pelt. But suddenly I felt the jolt of the next turn and saw the Russians racing past us parallel. Then we were off back across the field and safe. But that had done the job. Overtaken, the

The legend of the Stuka is closely associated with that of the Panzer. Stuka dive bombers provided devastatingly effective close support for the armoured formations. When the Germans launched their attack against the Stalin Line in June 1941, the 16th Panzer Division ran into Soviet artillery fire and suffered heavy casualties (*left, below left*) Stukas forced a break-in and once the ground troops were through the line they ranged ahead of the Panzers, attacking Soviet armour wherever it appeared. This photograph (*centre left*) shows what happens to a tank when it is hit by a bomb which detonates the ammunition. The fragments were once the components of a 46-ton KV-I tank./*Podzun Verlag*

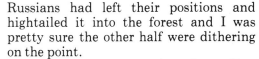

Russians had left their positions and hightailed it into the forest and I was pretty sure the other half were dithering on the point.

Suddenly I noticed Sea Rose Two coming in for the first time. But she wasn't barging down and blasting as she should have been. She was heading off the road in full retreat for cover. So the Russians hadn't been as dumb as we'd hoped. The road was now just one mass of smoke, the Russians and my two tanks blasting back at each other with everything they had. It was time for me to do my bit. Ordering Jochum to spin around completely to the south, I threw the lid of the turret open and stuck my head out so I could see more clearly. All the same, I made sure I kept hanging on for grim death to the sides. The Russians had no idea what was happening out on the field any more. We hadn't gone in, we hadn't retreated. We had just played cat and mouse with them like kids at a Sunday School picnic. Of the infantry and gunners still there, half were just standing around wondering what we or they were supposed to do next. I was hoping this might mean they were running out of ammunition.

We charged down towards them until we were right opposite Sea Rose Two. Then I saw the armoured car, Sea Rose Four — just one great roaring flame. Now we were completely surrounded by the Russians guns and Dita had our gun turret turning left, right and everywhere, firing continuously at anything and everything. Sea Rose Two came quickly back on to the main road and the three tanks moved down in line, our machine guns cross-spraying each other to keep the infantry off. We moved down towards the turn-off, gradually silencing every gun in the area. None of them was powerful enough to knock out a tank. The

Bottom left: Panzer and panzergrenadier divisions each had an anti-tank *Abteilung* equipped with 20mm Flak 38 guns. Each gun had a cyclic rate of fire of 400rpm and the four-barrelled gun — shown here mounted on a standard 1-ton half-track — was a most efficient weapon against low-flying attacks./*Podzun Verlag*

large columns retreating from the front had moved off the road altogether and into the forest at least a kilometre to escape us. They were making tracks out of there fast.

We now had the road from the north to the south and Odessa blocked and all that remained to resist us were the few left on the bridge road. Vehicles were burning, trees were burning, smoke was everywhere, and the infantry running wildly running towards the sea, making sure that under all circumstances they escaped this particular hot-spot. None of them cared. This small piece of Russia no longer interested them. An officer was waving his arms vainly and calling them back but none of them came.

Meanwhile, we still didn't know whether we were winning or losing the battle. Sea Rose Five hadn't come into the picture and I was sure it must have been hit. That left us only the three tanks.

Sea Rose Two was calling. "Captain, we're running out of gun ammunition."

"Okay." It was becoming hard for me to think clearly. I felt sick — I felt lousy. All I wanted was to get the hell out of Russia, Odessa, and everything connected with it, and lie on a nice soft bed and sleep. Had we won the battle or not? And when on earth were those *Das Reich* boys going to arrive. If they didn't get there soon, there just wouldn't be any of us left.

I braced my body against the side of the tank and asked Dita how many shots we had left. "Another ten, that's all," he told me. Sea Rose Three had only another three salvos so that settled that. None of us could afford to stay kicking around the highway any longer.

"Sea Rose Three," I called. "You and I will speed right to the turn-off. Now or never we will have to bluff it out. I'll go in front spraying the right-hand side of the highway, and you follow about twenty metres behind spraying the left-hand side. Leave yourself one shot. Sea Rose Two, head back to the forest and try and find out what happened to Number Five-then head back to Horst across the field as fast as your crawlers will carry you."

While we were amongst them the Russians couldn't even shoot for fear of blowing each other up, so all they could do against our onslaught was scatter to the sides of the road. But not so one Russian officer. We drove the tank straight for him but he still didn't budge. Alone on the emptied road, he waited unflinching for the moment when our tank would roll over him. Never had I felt so much for a Russian before. We turned the tank just before we reached him, drove past and down the bridge road. I didn't look behind but I knew he would still be there. As soon as we had turned, Dita swung his gun around to face the road and our last grenade was fired. Then at top speed we raced for the river. At

Left: A platoon of panzergrenadiers tramp through a street in the suburbs of Stalino in November 1941. The panzers reached the limit of their endurance about this time, and at the end of November 1941 the Russians launched a massive counter attack which forced the Germans back to the Mius river. In the winter of 1941/42 Stalino became the base of Panzer Army I./*Podzun Verlag*

least we had blocked the road and done enough damage to the Russians to keep them from recouping for an hour or so. I just hoped that by then our spearhead would have arrived.

Next came the job of crossing the infantry lines which had again reformed. But that was easily done. They were positioned on the south-west in a half-moon arc, but not only was there just the one row — they were again like ants in the field, lying everywhere. Our low machine gun was still intact and firing through, so they shifted out in a hurry. Then, to our right, we discovered an anti-tank gun facing the river. As they hadn't yet fired, I knew they must think we were Russians. Cursing that we had used our last shell, we blasted at the men behind the gun with machine gun fire. "Sea Rose Three?" I called. "Have you still got that one grenade?"

"As ordered, yes."

"Then blast that darned gun out of existence."

Sea Rose Two still had not emerged from the forest so I decided to call her up. She came in immediately. "The armoured car is a red mass of fire, captain. I'm on my way out and back to the river right now."

That was bad. It must somehow have got ahead of the other tanks or else been caught by a gun they had missed. Maybe the boys had managed to get out and save themselves. Maybe. But if even a quarter

of the Russians in that half-moon circle had been anything at all like their officer who stood on the road, they would have eaten not only them, but all of us, steel and men. I fired off a green rocket and received my answer from Horst. The Russian fire had petered out but on the west side of the river the tank brigade was still bombarding our side, though without effect.

I turned to watch the main road through my binoculars. Again the men were recouping; wave after wave of infantry were pouring out of the forest. I could see the burnt trucks being pushed off the road. The Russians must be

Above: Panzer units were usually refuelled and their ammunition replenished in the forward area. Whenever possible vehicles would be concentrated at forward rally points. But when panzers were tactically deployed in defensive positions, PoL would be brought up to them./*Podzun Verlag*

planning on getting heavier equipment, and if they did manage to get even one battery of heavy guns in there, they would pound us right out of the place. But then I remembered the Luftwaffe. Surely those planes had to return soon. As long as they could help us keep that heavy equipment out, particularly tanks and heavy artillery, we could keep the tank brigade boxed in. Our tank rolled in to Horst's position. He jumped up and poked his face into mine. "How was it up there?"

"Well, we ran through the infantry lines without being disturbed but as soon as we entered the forest in front of the highway, we ran into their blasted heavy anti-tank fire. We couldn't break through at that point so I sent two tanks and one armoured car in at high speed to crush everything in their way, while I had a happy time manoeuvring out on the field."

Right: A mine-lifting party of panzergrenadiers.

"I saw that — nearly died laughing too. Those Ruskies must have used up half the ammunition in Odessa lighting up the sky like fairyland for you — while you did exhibition dancing underneath."

"Ja! some fun. How's your position anyway."

"We'll be able to hold the brigade as long as the daylight lasts but don't ask me what might happen once the night arrives. It'll be just about impossible. I've got men posted in between the tanks to keep the Russian infantry from sneaking in but God knows — if there's no moon tonight . . ."

'Mine Dogs' against Panzer

Although British military experts have scoffed at the story that the Russians attacked German tanks by using dogs with mines strapped to their backs, it is in fact true and is substantiated by the archives of the Stalingrad Defence Museum, and by German sources.

In 1962, the German magazine *Kristall* published in some thirty instalments, an account of Hitler's attack on Russia under the title *Unternehmen Barbarossa* (Operation Barbarossa). It is a dramatic, and at times over-dramatised account, but it is correct in historical fact, though it is only one more attempt at an apologia. However, in the ninth instalment, describing the launching of the opening of Guderian's attack on 30 September 1941, the following story appears:

'On the morning of 30 September the simultaneous battles of Viasma and Briansk began with the roar of panzer cannon and anti-tank guns. The riflemen of the 1st Company, 3rd Rifle Regiment, cling like bunches of grapes to the troop-carriers. Why walk while there is no shooting? And the troop-carriers of the 1st Company can carry quite a number.

Up front Leutnant Lohse is travelling in the command truck of the 1st Company. "Look out for dogs, Eikmeier" he orders his driver.

"Dogs?" remarks the corporal. "Why watch out for dogs, Herr Leutnant?" Corporal Ostarek, the machine-gunner, also looks up surprised. "Dogs?" he says.

Lohse shrugs his shoulders. "Three Russian prisoners were handed over to the regiment yesterday. Each had dog. They said they were members of a Special Unit who led dogs carrying high explosive charges into action against tanks."

Living mines!

Ostarek laughs briefly. "That's as good an item of latrine news as I've ever heard," he said.

"If it hadn't been the regimental commander himself who warned Captain Peschke and me, I wouldn't have mentioned it," Lohse replied apologetically" "Anyway, you've been warned."

The trucks are driving across a broad field. Russian machine-gun fire can be heard on the left, from advanced positions along the edge of the sprawling village. The 3.7cm anti-tank guns open up. The riflemen of the 3rd Company have jumped off their carriers and advance on foot. Hand-grenades are being hurled into the wooden shacks. Near the church some well-camouflaged positions between the shacks come into view. Unteroffizier Dreger checks a party of Russians with his machine-gun.

Suddenly Eikmeier shouts, "A dog!"

The dog is running at top speed. On his back he carries a strange-looking saddle. Before Ostarek can bring his machine-gun into action, Captain Peschke has fired his rifle from the other side at 300 yards range. The dog leaps into the air and collapses, in a heap.

Suddenly Corporal Müller shouts, "Look out! Another one!"

A lovely alsatian dog approaches cautiously. Ostarek fires and misses. The dog lowers his tail and turns back . . .

"Radio was warning, Müller," Lohse orders. "Dora 10 . . . Attention everybody. Watch out for mine dogs!"

Mine dogs! A new word has been coined on the spur of the moment and it will go down in history as a new highly debatable weapon of the Soviets.

The dogs carried two linen saddle-bags filled with explosives. An upright wooden stick, four inches long, acted as a mechanical fuse. The dogs had been trained to run under the tanks and as soon as the stick bent or broke, the load on their backs exploded.

The 3rd Panzer Division did not suffer any losses in their encounter with these "living mines" of the Moscow Rifle Company, but two days later General Nehring's 18th Panzer Division were not so lucky . . .'

Soviet war literature does not mention this diabolical weapon but there is little doubt that mine-dogs were tried out. Interrogation of the captured dog-leaders by 3rd Panzer Division revealed that the Moscow Rifle Company was equipped with 108 dogs. They were trained with tractors. The dogs had to get their food from under tractors while the engines were running. If they refused they went hungry. They were hungry when brought into action and ran under the tanks where they hoped to find food.

Panther and Tiger Development

Left: The Panther was the most advanced German medium tank of the war. Its design was orientated around that of the famous Russian T-34, although many peculiarly German features — such as overlapping suspension — were incorporated. A Panther in Italy 1944 . . .

Right . . . and on the 'Invasion Front' in France 1944.

Panzerkampfwagen V (PzKpfw V)

During the first year of the war it was already apparent that the German panzers then in service or projected — the KpfwIs, IIs and IIIs — were not adequate to deal with the heavier French, British and Russian tanks. So in May 1941 Hitler decreed that his armies should be provided with new heavier fighting vehicles. In the event prototype 'heavy' tanks — which would now be classed as 'mediums' had already been developed.

From experiments with a vehicle they called the *Grosstraktor* the Germans had produced the PzKpfwV — a 35-ton vehicle fitted with a 75mm gun in one turret and two machine guns in another — and the PzKpfwVI, which had a 105mm gun. Both tanks had a crew of seven, which was considered uneconomic, and as their chassis proved to be defective they were rejected as unsatisfactory. (Although a few were built for propaganda purposes.)

Subsequently the new type of PzKpfwV, designated the *Panther*, was produced. Following a recommendation by experts who had made a thorough study of the Soviet T-34 which had created so much havoc on the Eastern front, the Daimler-Benz and MAN firms built two different prototype vehicles to take the 75mm gun currently being developed by Rheinmetall Borsig. The Wehrmacht preferred the MAN version but Hitler decided in favour of the Daimler-Banz. The first consignment reached the troops in mid-1943 and although there were set-backs with the original model the Panther became one of the most successful German tanks and one of the best of all those that appeared during World War II.

A 'Panther II' which was to have been fitted with a long 88mm gun in place of the 75mm weapon never got beyond the prototype stage.

Including different specialised versions (command, tank-recovery, mine-sweeping, etc) a total of 5,805 Panthers were built.

Characteristics of PzKpfw V Panther Ausf.G
Weight: 44.8 tonnes
Length (over hull): 6.88m
Length (over gun): 8.86m
Width: 3.43m
Height: 3.10m
Crew: 5
Thickest armour: 80mm
Engine: 700hp (Maybach 12-cylinder, water cooled)
Maximum road/cross country speed: 46/24kmph
Maximum range: 176km
Armament: 1 × 75mm KwK42 L70 gun
3 × 7.92mm MGs
3,740 Panther panzers were produced between 1943 and the end of the war.

Nomenclature of Variants on the Panther chassis
Artillery observation tank: *Beobachtungspanther* (with fixed turret and dummy gun)
Armoured recovery vehicle: *Bergepanther* (with no armament and open 'working' compartment)
Hunter-tank (tank-destroyer): *Jadgpanther*

Above: The *Jagdpanther* mounted the deadly 88mm Pak 43/3 L/71 gun. 230 were built and nearly all of them were sent to the Eastern Front. This is one of the few which went to France (1944).

Below: Tiger I in Tunisia 1943 . . .

Right: . . . . and in Russia 1942.

Panzerkampfwagen VI (PzKpfw VI) 'Tiger'

The 'Tiger' was perhaps the most famous and spectacular heavy tank of the war. Built to a specification which required the new panzer to find its target at 1,500m and penetrate 10mm of armour plate, prototypes were submitted by Henschel and Porsche. The former got the order, and in August 1942 started production of the PzKpfwVI which was first called 'Tiger Model E' and later simply 'Tiger I'. Like the Panther the Tiger was rushed into service too early and there were many teething troubles. All too often the giant Tiger broke down, and because her great bulk made her difficult to manoeuvre the Germans nicknamed her the 'Furniture Van'. In action the sheer weight (57 tons) of its massive turret meant a slow traverse of the outstanding and famous 88mm gun with which it was equipped. But this gun gave it almost unrivalled hitting power and British troops in Tunisia were overawed by the giant Tiger when they met her late in 1942.

By November 1942 only 13 Tigers had been built but after that production reached 25 or more a month. Total output of Tiger I was 1,350. The first saw action before Leningrad in September 1942, and others were subsequently employed in North Africa and Italy, and — towards the end of the war — on all the fronts round Germany.

Right: Tiger I in Russia in 1942...

Below ...and in 1943.

Characteristics of PzKpfw VI Ausf.E.
Tiger I (Sd Kfz 181)
Weight: 55 tonnes
Length (over hull): 6.20m
Length (over gun): 8.24m
Width: 3.73m
Height: 2.86m
Crew: 5
Thickest Armour: 110mm (turret)
Engine: 700hp (Maybach 12-cylinder,
      water cooled)
Maximum road/cross
   country speed: 46/24kmph
Maximum range: 100km
Armament: 1 × 88mm KwK 36 gun
         2 MGs
         6 smoke dischargers

On 1 August 1943 a leaflet describing the new Tiger was published under General Guderian's signature. 'With two fingers', he said, 'You can shift 700hp, move 60 tons, drive at 45kmph on the road or 20kmph across country, and cross a water obstacle four metres deep... On the southern sector of the Russian front in one six hour engagement a Tiger was hit 227 times by anti-tank rifle shots, besides receiving fourteen hits by 52mm shells and eleven by 76.2mm projectiles — none of which penetrated the armour. The road wheels were shot to pieces, two torsion bars were knocked out, several anti-tank missiles were jammed in the transmission, and the tank had run over three mines. Yet it managed to run another 60km across country... You can destroy a T-34 at 800 metres, but the T-34 needs to get to within 500 metres of you if you are in a Tiger!'

To this eulogy it is relevant to add that the complicated construction of a single Tiger entailed 300,000 man-hours of work — which explains its high cost of production (800,000 Reichs Marks).

Above left: Cleaning the muzzle-brake of the Tiger's 88mm gun. Russia 1942.

Left: The Porsche-Tiger Jagdpanzer Ferdinand or Elefant shown here was a cross between tank destroyer and self-propelled gun — mounting the 88mm anti-tank 43L/71 gun on the chassis of the giant Porsche Tiger. Weighing 73 tons and carrying 102/120mm of armour at the front and 82mm on the side the Russians soon showed that the Elefant could be knocked out by a Molotov cocktail lobbed on to the engine compartment. This photograph of a disabled Elefant was taken in Italy in 1944.

Right: The concrete like appearance of the armour surface was created by the application of a special paste to counter magnetic and sticky mines.

Below: PzKpfw VI, Tiger II, *Königstiger* had much thicker armour and a more powerful gun (the 88mm KwK 43 L/71 in place of the 88mm KwK 36 L/56 on the Tiger I).

Panzerkampfwagen VI 'Tiger II'

The Panthers and Tiger Is were more than a match for individual Russian tanks in 1943. Nevertheless the Germans felt the need for heavier and better vehicles, and in August 1944 the superb Tiger II, or *Königstiger* (Royal Tiger) came into service. Weighing 68 tons in battle order it was the heaviest tank to fight in World War II. Its 88mm L/71 gun, thick sloped armour, ease of maintenance, and the arrangement of the crew positions made it not only one of the most powerful tanks of the war, but with the Germans one of the most popular. By March 1945 however only 485 Royal Tigers were ready for action and consequently another of Hitler's 'war winners' could not do much good.

Characteristics of PzKpfw VI Tiger II, Königstiger (SdKfz 182)
Weight: 70 tonnes
Length (over hull): 7.26m
Length (over gun): 10.26m (33ft 9in)
Width: 3.75m
Height: 3.10m
Crew: 5
Thickest Armour: 185mm (turret)
Engine: 600-700hp (Maybach 12-cylinder, water cooled)
Maximum road/cross country speed: 42/17kmph
Maximum Range: 110km
Armament: 1 × 8.8cm KwK 43/L71 gun
　　　　　　2 MGs

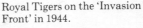

Royal Tigers on the 'Invasion Front' in 1944.

Jagdpanzer VI, 'Jagdtiger' (SdKfz 186)

By mounting the massive 128mm L/55 gun on a modified Tiger chassis, the Germans created the *Jagdtiger* anti-tank assault gun. Both Henschel and Porsche produced a few such vehicles to their own design. Because they arrived on the scene late in the day only 48 were produced. In consequence the *Jagdtiger* tank destroyers, like the Royal Tiger tanks, had no effect on the outcome of the war although they overawed those who saw them in battle. At about 76 tonnes the *Jagdtiger* was the heaviest of the World

War II armoured vehicles, and its 250mm thick armour made it virtually invulnerable to anti-tank fire. Mechanically however it was unreliable and the *Jagdtigers* were of little practical use except as mobile anti-tank pillboxes.

With its forward turret mounting the *Jagdtiger* manufactured by Henschel was easily distinguished from that produced by Porsche, whose engine and high box turret were at the rear. The latter (SdKfz 184s) were first nicknamed 'Ferdinand' (the forename of the designer Porsche) and later 'Elefant'.

91

Below: Refurbishing a Royal
Tiger, France 1944.

Bottom: A Royal Tiger awaiting
recovery. The spare track links
and 'extras' have all been
removed. Spares were short in 1944.

The Porsche Superpanzer

In 1943 Hitler commissioned Porsche to produce an extravagantly heavy superpanzer *Maus* and two prototypes were built the following year. Known in the factory as 'The Travelling Bunker', the two *Maus* tanks each weighed 189 tons, and were fitted with 1,200hp engines that should have given them a top speed of 20kmph. Armament was a 128mm cannon which fired shells weighing 120 or 155lbs and recoiled about a metre. Turrets weighed about 50 tons, measured three metres across and the air-cooling systems required 150hp. The *Maus* could only be transported by rail on a special wagon, and as hardly any bridges could carry such a load it was designed to ford waterways up to seven and a half metres deep.

Hitler attended a demonstration of one of these monsters, which rolled half-way across a field and then broke down. A few months later both of these 'superpanzers' were blown up to prevent their capture by the advancing Russians.

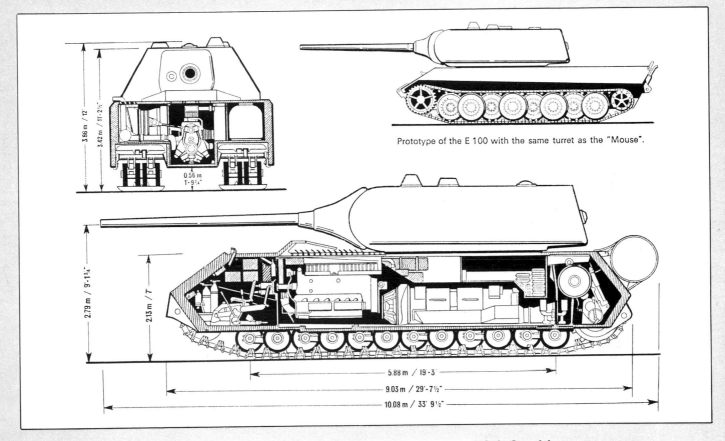

Prototype of the E 100 with the same turret as the "Mouse".

Left: One of the two superpanzer *Maus* prototypes. /Motorbuch Verlag

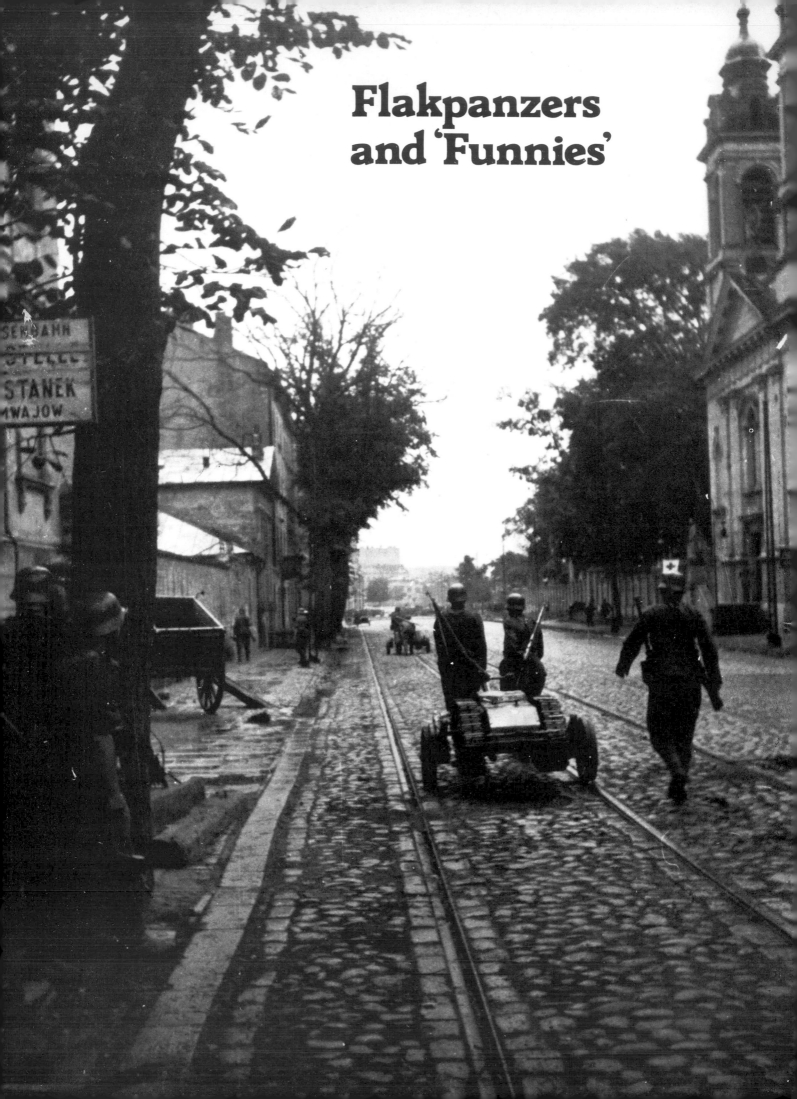

Flakpanzers and 'Funnies'

Far left: Goliath was a remote
controlled explosive device,
which was first used in Operation
Citadel near Kursk in 1943.
Designed as a miniature tank and
carrying an explosive load of 91kg
Goliath was directed to its targets
by radio installed in another
tracked vehicle. Because of its
low speed it was suitable only for
use against static targets. The
photograph was taken in a
Warsaw street during the
abortive rising in August 1944.

Above: Goliath's control unit.
(Photographs of these devices are
rather rare. This one was taken
during field trials.)

Centre left: Panzer divisions had
their own Anti-Aircraft artillery,
mounted on tank chassis so that
they could keep up in an advance.
One of the earliest was the FLA-
Kreuzer — twin 20mm Oerlikon
guns in a closed turret.

Bottom left: The Flakvierling 38
on a PzKpfw IV chassis was
produced in a variety of forms.
All had quadruple mountings.
With an open fighting
compartment.

Above: With a semi-closed turret . . .

Above right: . . . . and as a turreted pattern, *Wirbelwind*.

Centre right: The heaviest self-propelled Flakpanzer was the 88mm Flak 37.

Bottom right: The *Möbelwagen* (Furniture Van) was similar to the *Wirbelwind*, and equipped with 37mm AA guns.

Far right, top: And one of the 14th Motorised Infantry Division (Panzergrenadiers) in the Ukraine in 1943.

Far right, bottom: The *Kettenkrad* (motor cycle tractor). Capable of crossing almost every kind of terrain and carrying a useful load, they were employed extensively as communications vehicles.

97

The Offensive that was to end the War

A *Panzerspähwagen* (armoured car with special communications equipment) and an armoured personnel carrier mounting a 20mm gun carrying the symbol of the Kleist Group. Pairs of vehicles like these were used for long range reconnaissance missions (rather like the British Long Range Desert Group patrols). To control the gap created between the Terek and Volga Rivers the 16th Motorised Infantry Division organised a special long range reconnaissance troop. Starting in September (1942) from Elista the three groups of this troop drove many hundreds of kilometres on missions which took them as far afield as the Caspian Sea, Astrakhan and the lower Volga.

By the end of 1941 the battle-weary panzer units which had taken part in Operation Barbarossa were no longer fit to fight. Fortunately no mobile operations were envisaged during the Russian winter, even if they had been possible, or in the spring of 1942 when the melting snow turned the ground once more into a morass. Consequently most of the panzer divisions were pulled out and transferred to France, to rest, reorganize and re-train while in Germany more panzer divisions were being raised, and motorised divisions converted into panzergrenadier divisions.

Meanwhile Hitler was pondering on the next phase of the war. There was no question of being able to resume the attack along the whole front again, and the generals suggested to the Führer that perhaps it might be better to stay on the defensive. By doing so the Russians might well batter themselves to pieces in a series of frustrating and exhausting offensives. Hitler rejected the idea; he believed that Russia must be 'knocked out' before Britain and America opened a second front, and as he feared that this might happen in 1943 he ruled that the offensive must be resumed in 1942. In Führer Directive No 41 issued in April 1942 he laid down the objectives. In the north Leningrad had to be captured. But the primary objective was a thrust in the south, a break-through into the

Above: Cleaning the weapon ports of a Tiger I, Russia 1942.

Right: A disabled Tiger I, Russia 1942.

ORGANISATION OF THE PANZERTROOPS ON JULY 9TH 1942

B
WEICHS

DON (AB 20.11)
v MANSTEIN

A
LIST / v KLEIST

8 (ITL.)   3 (RUM)   6 PAULUS   4 HOTH   I v. KLEIST   2 (UNG.)   17

XXXXVIII   XIV   XXXX   LVII   XXIV

3   9   11   14   16   17   22   23   24

3   16   29   60   G.D   SS-W

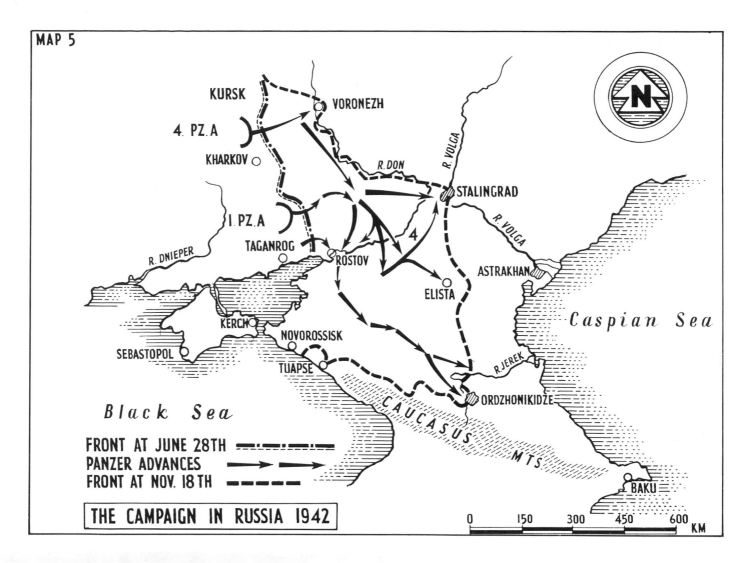

MAP 5

KURSK   VORONEZH

4. PZ.A

KHARKOV

R. DON   R. VOLGA

STALINGRAD

I. PZ.A

R. DNIEPER   TAGANROG

ROSTOV   4

R. VOLGA

ASTRAKHAN

ELISTA

Caspian Sea

KERCH

SEBASTOPOL   NOVOROSSISK

TUAPSE   R. JEREK

ORDZHONIKIDZE

Black Sea   CAUCASUS MTS

FRONT AT JUNE 28TH —·—·—
PANZER ADVANCES ———▶
FRONT AT NOV. 18TH ———

BAKU

THE CAMPAIGN IN RUSSIA 1942

0   150   300   450   600   KM

Caucasus; the capture of Moscow could wait until the Caucasus oil fields were in German hands.

The Caucasus operation was entrusted to Army Group South, and nearly all the Wehrmacht's available panzer units were assigned to the two Panzer Armies — First and Fourth — that were to spearhead the advance. By May most of the panzer divisions involved were up to about eighty five per cent of their original fighting strength, and had been equipped with PzKpfw IIIs and IVs. Apart from the great rivers Donetz, Don, Volga and Terek, the Caucasus area was ideal tank country, and the panzers were expected to chop through the Russians just as they had done in the previous summer. The offensive was scheduled to begin on 28 June, after the Russians still holding out in the Kerch peninsula and the Crimea had been mopped up, and a large enemy penetration near Kharkov eliminated.

The capture of the Kerch Peninsula and the fortress of Sebastopol was carried out by General von Manstein during the course of May and June — for which he was rewarded with a marshal's baton. All was now ready for the main operation to get under way. Before it could do so, however, the Russians launched their own offensive — driving into the middle of the German Sixth Army threatening the main German supply base at Kharkov. In the event the offensive was brought to a halt when the First Panzer Army under General von Kleist, counter-attacked the flanks of the bulge created by the Russian advance. And on 22 May, when the 14th Panzer Division linked up with the Sixth Army and the Soviet salient was nipped off, two Russian Armies were encircled. Fighting in opposite directions the two Soviet armies tried in vain to break the ring, and there was some bloody fighting which ended in a German victory and the capitulation of 240,000 Russian troops. The panzer war of 1942 appeared to have started well, and it was not yet in full swing.

At the end of June (1942), while Field Marshal Rommel was grouping his panzers for the drive against the British defences at El Alamein, Army Group South under Field Marshal von Bock launched the Caucasus offensive. Spearheaded by 15 panzer and panzergrenadier divisions of the First and Fourth Panzer Armies, Italian, Hungarian, Rumanian and German formations began their attack on 28 June. Two days later, 150km further south, two panzer divisions and one panzergrenadier division began the second phase of the offensive when they veered north to cut off the Russian troops around Voronezh. On this occasion however, partly because Hitler changed von Bock's orders and partly because Stalin had issued instructions for more elastic Russian tactics, most of the Russian troops the Germans had expected to trap in the customary fashion escaped. The town of Voronezh itself fell on 7 July; by then the panzers, had got as far as the Don, and *Grossdeutschland* panzergrenadiers had established a bridgehead on the far bank.

In accordance with the original plan the two panzer armies now began to converge on Stalingrad, and both were making good progress when Hitler intervened with another change of plan. The pincer movement on Stalingrad was to be abandoned, he ordered. He was convinced that — with Soviet Russia at the end of its tether (as he then believed) — the Russian forces retiring before the panzers on the Don could be enveloped between the Don and the Donetz. They could then be destroyed in one great battle before they had a chance to retreat

Right: Panzer on the march . . . taken in Russia in 1942, showing that tanks form only a relatively small proportion of the vehicles in panzer and panzergrenadier divisions. The photograph shows armoured personnel carriers of the *Grossdeutschland* Division./*Podzun Verlag*

Below: PzKpfw III and panzergrenadiers of the 4th Panzer Army in Stalingrad. The grain silo in the southern suburbs of Stalingrad became a symbol of Soviet resistance. On 22 September 1942 a battalion of Russian infantry was totally annihilated inside this silo. It was sacrificed in order to give General Chuykov an opportunity to organise another defensive line further north.

102

via Rostov towards the Caucasus. It was wishful thinking; nevertheless the panzers were ordered to abandon the advance on Stalingrad and embark on an encirclement operation for a battle which never took place. Under the new plan the Sixth Army was to go on to capture Stalingrad without the panzers, the First Panzer Army was to swing down towards Rostov and the lower reaches of the Don, and for a while the Fourth Panzer Army was kept standing at the Don bridgehead held by the *Grossdeutschland* panzergrenadiers.

The German front was already some 500km long and 200-400km deep, and the German panzer divisions of the First Panzer Army were rapidly swallowed up by the vastness of the Ukrainian steppes. However on 22 July the leading troops of the III and LVII Panzer Corps arrived on the outskirts of Rostov and, although there was some fierce street fighting before the city fell, there was no real resistance. The Russians were already well on their way back towards the Caucasus in full retreat, and there was no

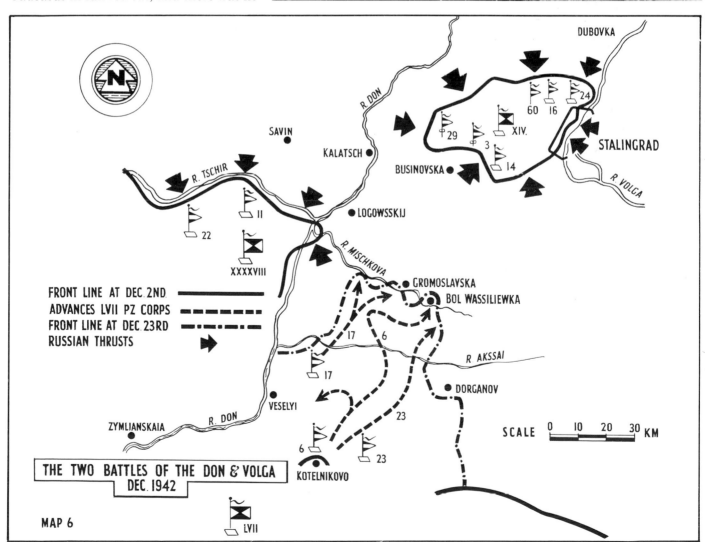

FRONT LINE AT DEC. 2ND. ——————
ADVANCES LVII PZ CORPS – – – – – –
FRONT LINE AT DEC. 23RD –·–·–·–·–
RUSSIAN THRUSTS ➤

THE TWO BATTLES OF THE DON & VOLGA DEC. 1942

MAP 6

SCALE 0 10 20 30 KM

Left: A disabled PzKpfw IV of the 1st SS-Panzer Division *Leibstandarte Adolf Hitler* in Kharkov, autumn 1943. During the years 1941, 1942 and 1943 Karkov was taken by the Germans, retaken by the Russians, taken back by the Germans, and then finally retaken by the Russians. When this photograph was taken the Germans were holding it for the second time. Gefreiter Guy Sajer recalls: 'The town looked like a jumble of burnt-out wreckage. Acres of total destruction had been used as dumps for the piles of wrecked machinery of every kind which the occupying troops had collected in their efforts to clear the roads. This mass of twisted torn metal reflected the ferocious violence of battle. It was all too easy to imagine the fate of the combatants. Motionless beneath the shroud of snow which partially covered them, these steel cadavers marked a stage in the war . . .'

longer any question of the 'encirclement' battle envisaged by the Führer.

The first major objectives in the 1942 summer offensive had been achieved and the rapid advance of the German panzers had set new records in armoured warfare. But no Russian armies had been captured at Voronezh or in the bend of the Don River; so the German successes were Pyrrhic victories. Although the panzers had driven their machines and themselves to the limit, they had not been able to repeat the successes of 1941. The law of diminishing returns had come into play: the further the panzers advanced, the more extended the front and greater the logistics problems.

On 30 July units of the 3rd Panzer Division crossed the Manych River and headed south towards the oil fields between Batum and Baku. They were now in Asia, where the parched terrain, steppe grass, water shortages, and temperatures of 50°C posed a whole new set of problems. Moving in isolation across the steppes the Division's only contact with other German units back near the Don was by radio and light aircraft. In a week the 3rd Division Panzers covered 400km, and on 25 August they occupied Mosdok; two days later when they captured a bridge over the Terek River, they reached the limit of the German thrust into Asia. By this time they had outrun their supply lines, and the vehicles bringing up fuel were using more petrol than they could transport. Camels were pressed into service and camel caravans organised. But it was not enough. The Russians were bringing fresh

troops across the Caspian Sea to reinforce their army defending the Caucasus oilfield. Under constant attack 3 Panzer Division was compelled to turn back. The advance was over.

Stalingrad

The battle of Stalingrad was the direct outcome of one of Hitler's changes of objective. Stalingrad was of secondary importance when the 1942 summer offensive was planned, but the deviation imposed on the original plan by the Führer led to a tremendous battle of attrition, involving 21 German divisions — including six panzer and panzergrenadier divisions.

The attack started on 23 August, and within two days panzers of the 6th Panzer Division penetrated to the western banks of the Volga and the northern outskirts of the city. Here the Russian defenders stubbornly resisted any further advance. The new Soviet commander of the 62nd Army, General Chuikov, having been told that his men had to fight 'to the last bullet', every factory and every house in every street became a veritable fortress. In the northern suburbs the fighting was some of the bloodiest in the whole war, with the Russians at a definite disadvantage because their reinforcements had to be ferried across the Volga and this could only be done at night. By the beginning of November, as the Russian winter freeze set in, the Germans had managed to push Chuikov's men back into a few hundred square yards of factory buildings. Then the Russians counterattacked.

Clearly planned and timed to coincide with both the frost which enabled tanks to move cross-country and the opening of the Allied landings in North Africa, four army groups under Marshal Zhukov launched a double encircling operation against the Germans crowded in and around Stalingrad. The Soviet Voronezh, South-West and Don Armies slashed in from the north of the city while the Stalingrad Army attacked from the south; following the Russian armour came great bodies of cavalry. The Fourth Panzer Army was split in two, the overextended German lines gave way and the trap closed around the Sixth Army on 22 November. Von Paulus, its commander, asked for permission to break out of the pocket. But the Führer ordered him to hold on — promising to airlift 500 tons supplies daily, and rushing von Manstein from the Leningrad front to the newly founded Army Group Don with orders to retrieve and stabilize the situation.

As the Sixth Army's position deteriorated, with the Luftwaffe delivering a daily average of only about 70 tons of supplies, von Manstein hurriedly reorganised three understrength panzer divisions and threw them into a relief operation. By 19 Dec the 6th Panzer Division had fought its way to within 50km of Stalingrad, and von Manstein ordered von Paulus to break out. But von Paulus, waiting for Hitler's authorisation, hesitated until suddenly the front held by the 8th Italian Army collapsed.

At this point under the increasing pressure of the Soviet offensive 6 Panzer Division and the remnants of the Fourth Panzer Army were compelled to retreat, leaving the Sixth Army in the encircled city to its fate. There was now no hope of relief and on 2 February 1943 the last of the German troops — 90,000 men — surrendered. With them went the 14th, 16th and 24th Panzer Divisions, and the 3rd, 29th and 60th Panzergrenadier Divisions which ceased to exist.

Winter 1943

Obergefreiter Lenson recalls:

'One night, the Russians sent a human wave of Mongols in a direct assault against our positions. Their function was to knock out the minefield, by crossing it. As the Russians preferred to economise on tanks, and as their human stockpile was enormous, they usually sent out men for jobs of this kind.

The Soviet attack failed; the minefield exploded under the howling mob, and we sent out a curtain of yellow and white fire to obliterate anyone who had survived. The fragmented corpses froze very quickly sparing us the stench which would otherwise have polluted the air over a vast area.

The Russians had not even used any of their artillery to help the Mongols, which seemed to confirm our estimate of the situation. We sent out patrols to try to remine the field, but the Russians were ready to fire on anything that moved. We were able to put down only a light sprinkling of mines, with regrettably heavy losses. It was clearly no longer possible to rely on mines to protect our front line.

On another evening, when the cold had attained a dramatic intensity, the Russians attacked again. We were manning our positions in a temperature which had dropped to 45° below zero. Some men fainted when the cold struck them, paralysed before they even had a chance to scream. Survival seemed almost impossible. Our hands and faces

Bottom left: Servicing a Sturmgeschütz at a field workshop. Gefreiter Guy Sajer of the 17th Light Infantry Battalion, *Grossdeutschland* Division, recalls: 'Winter 1942 seemed endless. It snowed every day, almost without a break. I remember we were taken by rail to a town used as a medical centre, some fifty miles from Kharkov. Food, blankets, medicines and other supplies were stored in big sheds, and every cellar and hole in the ground was jammed with munitions. There were also repair shops — some indoors, others in the open air. Soldiers perching on tanks blew on their fingers when they grew too numb to hold a wrench. A system of trenches and strong points had been organised on the outskirts of the town. This part of the country suffered from frequent partisan attacks, often by large groups of men. Wherever this happened every mechanic and warehouseman abandoned his tools and inventories for a machine gun to protect the supplies and himself . . .'

Above: Russian 'Rasputitza'! A PzKpfw V (Panther) towed by a recovery vehicle...

were coated with engine grease, and when our worn gloves were pulled over this gluey mixture, every gesture became extremely difficult. Our tanks, whose engines would no longer start, swept the spaces in front of them with their long tubes, like elephants caught in a trap.

The mujiks preparing to attack us were suffering in the same way, freezing where they stood before there was time for even one *"Ourrah pobieda"* [Hurrah Victory!]. The men on both sides, suffering a common martyrdom, were longing to call it quits. Metal broke with astonishing ease. The Soviet tanks advanced blindly in the light of flares, which intensified the bluish gliter of the scene. These tanks were destroyed by the mines which lay parallel to our trenches some thirty yards from our front line, or by our Tigers, which fired without moving. The Russian troops, with frozen hands and feet, faltered and withdrew in confusion in the face of the fire we kept steady, despite our tortured hands. Their officers, who had hoped to find us paralysed by cold and incapable of defence, were unconcerned about the condition of their own troops. They were ready to make any sacrifice, so long as our lines were attacked.

I managed to keep my hands from freezing by thrusting them, in their gloves, into two empty ammunition boxes, when the cartridges had run into the spandau. Our gunners, and everyone forced to use his hands, sooner or later turned up at the medical service with severe cases of freezing. There were a great many amputations.

The intense cold lasted for three weeks, during which the Russians restricted themselves to sending over music calculated to make us homesick, and speeches inviting us to surrender.

Toward the end of January, the cold lessened somewhat, and became tolerable. At times during the day the thermometer rose as high as five degrees above zero. The nights were still murderous, but with frequent shifts of duty we managed to get through them. We knew that the Russian offensive would soon resume. One night, or rather one morning, toward four or five o'clock, blasts of the whistle sent us out once again to our interception posts.

A mass of T-34 tanks were moving forward. An artillery bombardment had preceded them, inflicting heavy damage on Boporoeivska, and provoking a mass evacuation by the civilian population,

which had been waiting for the fighting in terrified apprehension. Our tanks — about fifteen Tigers, ten Panthers, and a dozen PzIIs and PzIIIs — had managed to start their engines, which had been heated continuously the day before. At the beginning of the offensive, two PzIIs had been destroyed side by side in the Russian bombardment. The front was once again threatening to give way. We lay in our trenches and waited for the hordes of Red infantry which were usually not long in coming. For the moment our machine guns and *Panzerfausts* were quiet, leaving the way clear for our heavy artillery and our tanks.

Meantime the camouflaged Tigers waited with their engines idling. Almost every time a Russian tank came into range, a sharp strident burst set it on fire. The Russians were moving toward us slowly, sure of themselves, firing at random. Their tactic of demoralization would have worked if there had not been so many plumes of black smoke rising against the pale February sky. Our 37s and *Panzerfausts,* designed to be used at almost point-blank range, were scarcely called on. The first wave of Soviet armour was consumed five hundred yards from our first positions, nailed down by the concentrated fire of our Tigers and Panthers and heavy anti-tank guns.

The Tiger was an astonishing fortress. Enemy fire seemed to have almost no effect on its shell, which, at the front was five and a half inches thick. Its only weakness was its relative immobility.

A second Russian wave followed closely after the first, more dense than the first, and accompanied by a swarm of infantry which posed a serious threat.

We waited, dry-mouthed, our guns jammed against our shoulders and our grenades in easy reach. Our hearts were pounding.

Suddenly like a miracle, thirty of our planes flew over. As promised, the squadron from Vinnitsa was attacking. This particular job was easy for them, and every bomb hit home.

A cry of *"Sieg Heil, der Luftwaffe",* rang so loudly from our trenches that the pilots might almost have heard it. We opened fire with everything we had, but the Russian offensive kept coming, despite overwhelming losses. Our tanks drove at the stricken enemy with an ardour worthy of 1941.

The noise became unbearable. The air was thick with bitter fumes and smoke, and the smells of gunpowder and burned

107

gasoline. Our shouts mingled with the shouts of the Russians, who were reeling under the unexpected resistance.

We were able to watch the magnificent progress of our Tigers, pulverizing the enemy tanks before they were able to complete a half-turn. The Luftwaffe attacked again with rockets and 20mm cannons. The Russian rout was hidden by a thick curtain of luminous smoke.

The Russian artillery kept on firing at our lines, causing several deaths which we scarcely noticed. However, their guns were soon overrun by their own retreating troops, and fell silent.

A second wave of German planes, an undreamed-of extra luxury, completed the Russian debacle. We hugged each other in excitement, bursting with joy.

For a year now, we had been retreating before an enemy whose numerical superiority was constantly increasing.

In our sector all the lines had held, and we felt very proud. We had proved once again that with adequate material and a certain minimum preparation we could hold told off an enemy of greatly superior size, whose frenzied efforts were never intelligently employed.

One veteran, Wiener, had often remarked on this Russian failing at difficult moments. At the sight of an enemy tank in flames, he would bare his teeth in a wide grin and say "What a damed fool to let himself caught like that. It's only their numbers that will get us eventually."

There were thirty Iron Crosses for us after this action . . .'

Tiger pill-box

Heinz Schröter writes:

'Vehicles which could not be recovered or repaired in situ, whose armament was still functioning, were sometimes used as pill-box strong points. One such tank of the 24th Panzer Division became a focal point of defence in the final days of Stalingrad. Until it was immobilised this tank had been used by one of the 24th Division's regimental commanders, and it was linked by field telephone to Divisional HQ. But it could neither move nor be moved. However the armour was sound, the turret could be closed, and the interior offered a modicum of comfort as well as security to five panzergrenadiers as the German perimeter shrank. Taking cover inside the panzer they slammed the turret shut, as Russian troops sped past.

Within an hour they found themselves 2 km behind the Russian front, completely cut off and with little hope of rejoining the comrades.

But there was some food in the tank; they found that both the tank's gun and its machine gun worked, and there was plenty of ammunition for both. Moreover when one of the five picked up the field telephone and gave the handle a tentative turn, an operator at the divisional exchange answered him.

"What are we supposed to do?", the panzergrenadier asked.

"Stay where you are", was the answer.

For a week the five panzergrenadiers lay doggo. Then a Russian patrol discovered their presence and a company of infantry mounted an attack on their hideout. The Russians were allowed to get within 50 metres before they opened fire with the tank machine gun and drove them off. A 24 hour respite followed, before the Russians attacked again — this time with tanks. When they were repulsed for the second time the panzergrendiers were able to report to Divisional HQ that they had knocked out three T-34s. After that the battle for what the Germans in Stalingrad were calling 'Command Post 506' raged incessantly — with the Russians bringing up more T-34s and using first mortars and then artillery. Clearly this situation could not continue: with the machine-gun ammunition, food and water supplies exhausted, and only very few rounds remaining for the 75mm gun, the senior of the five panzergrenadiers picked up the field telephone and asked Divisional HQ what they were supposed to do next.

"Remember what the Russians did when they were pinned down in the Silo", advised the officer who replied.

It was cold comfort: the Russians in the Silo had fought on until they were annihilated, but a Russian prisoner captured later in another part of Stalingrad had told the Germans that when they ran out of food their commander had radioed that if they fought harder they would not feel hungry. Finally when the men in the Silo ran out of ammunition, he had sent a last message: "The Soviet Union thanks you; your sacrifice has not been in vain."

Nothing more was heard of the panzergrenadiers after they reported that CP506 was being attacked by flame-throwers. Germany did not thank them, and it is doubtful whether their deaths fulfilled any useful purpose either,!

Italy

PzKpfw II Ausf.G in front of a Tiger.

Some weeks before the end of hostilities in North Africa the Allies had begun planning the invasion of Italy, and in July 1943 three British divisions of the British Eighth Army and three divisions of the American Seventh Army were put ashore on Sicily.

Axis forces in Sicily comprised four Italian infantry divisions, one of which was motorised, six coast guard divisons of doubtful reliability, and about 75,000 Germans. The majority of the latter were administrative troops, but they also included 15 Panzergrenadier Division under General Rodt and the *Herman Göring* Panzer Division. Both divisions were somewhat green and under-strength — 15th Panzer Division having only just been reconstituted after its gruelling experiences in North Africa. Between them the two divisions had about 160 tanks, and, at the time of the Allied landing, both divisions were officially designated as the Italian Commander-in-Chief's mobile reserve.

The Allied invasion was preceded by a massive sea and air bombardment, which quickly suppressed any fire in the bellies of the Italian Coast Guards. In consequence the sea assault was completely successful and the British force which landed on the south-east corner of the island was able to move quickly inland. The Americans who had landed on the south coast did not fare so well, however. The *Herman Göring* panzers had only two battalions of tanks — about 100 in all — including 17 of the new Tigers. And

Top left: The vehicle in the foreground (leading a file of Panthers) is said to be a demolition vehicle.

Centre left: Brummbär (Grizzly Bear) — a 150mm howitzer on a PzKpfw IV chassis. Only about 60 of these assault guns were built. They were used by the infantry gun companies of the Panzer divisions.

Bottom left: Tiger I. Replacing a track of this size was an exhausting task.

Below: Panthers of the 16th Panzer Division in Rome.

Left: 'While stands the Coliseum, Rome shall stand.'

Below: 75mm Assault Gun (on PzKpfw IV chassis) serving as an observation post.

Right: Replacing a track under fire. A PzKpfw IV on the Gustav Line. This was probably a Panzer of the 29th Panzergrenadier Division *Hermann Göring*.

Below: Concealed Panther 'somewhere' in Italy 1944.

when *Hermann Göring's* soldiers launched a counter-attack the Americans were driven right back to the beaches, despite the fact that some of the panzergrenadiers who had never been in action before are said to have fled from the scene of the battle crying 'hysterically'. (This display brought a stern order from the divisional commander, General Paul Conrath, who threatened 'severest measures ... cowardice punished on the spot ... death sentences.' It also brought General Rodt's panzergrenadiers from the north-east of the island to relieve the *Hermann Göring* Division, and for two weeks the American advance was delayed. But Allied pressure was growing and the Italians showed little desire to fight.) The XIV Panzer Corps comprising 29 Panzergrenadier Division and the 1st Parachute Division (FschJgDiv) were brought in to hold the line while the German installations and base troops were evacuated to the mainland. In the event despite the great preponderance of Allied air power, the tenacious resistance of the panzers and paratroops covered the successful exodus of more than 100,000 men, 9,800 vehicles and 50 tanks before the Allies occupied Messina.

Sicily had shown that the Italians were tired of war and had no wish to see their country turned into a battlefield. General Conrath's order to his panzergrenadiers, relayed to other German units, steadied the Wehrmacht troops and the Germans in Italy fought with their customary stubborn determination. But not even threats could stiffen the Italians. Mussolini was deposed on 25 July and although officially Italy was still allied to Germany, it was already clear that the Wehrmacht would have to bear the brunt of any fighting in Italy. The nature of the

Italian terrain was generally not suited to aggressive mobile operations — even if other factors had not ruled them out. Rommel was all for pulling out immediately and returning to a defensive line in the Apennines, but Hitler flatly refused. So the German High Command sent more troops to Italy, and by doing so behaved precisely as the Allies wished, for troops engaged in Italy obviously could not fight elsewhere. The divisions which had got away from Sicily were reorganised and reinforced, and reconstituted into the Tenth Army; (the 15th Panzergrenadier Division which had suffered heavy losses was one of thse divisions). Additionally the LXXVI Panzer Korps, which included the 16 and 26 Panzer Divisions, was sent to support Tenth Army.

It is not proposed to recount the story of the campaign in Italy. Events moved quickly in the early stages of the Allied invasion. German resistance was skilfully conducted and the role played by the panzers was professional and tenacious. But all they could do was to slow the Allied rate of advance. At Salerno, for example — where 16 Panzer Division was allotted a 48km sector to defend — there was never any hope of preventing the landing and although the Germans inflicted heavy losses on the Allies the Tenth Army could not muster enough men to drive the British and Americans back into the sea.

Panzers were deployed in the Gustav Line and subsequently in the Gothic Line, but mostly in static positions; Panthers, Tigers and a variety of assault guns became mobile gun emplacements. Their use as such bolstered German resistance and prolonged the campaign. But their value now was tactical; as strategic assets they had no value in Italy.

Above: This captured British Bren Carrier has been pressed into service with a mobile tank-hunting squad. (Note the *Panzerfausts*, and the fact that the squad included a medical orderly.)

The Beginning of the End

Normandy

The Allied Invasion of France on 6 June 1944 was the emotional and the strategic climax of the war. The Germans knew that it was coming, and for many months — spurred on by the dynamic panzer hero of North Africa, Rommel — soldiers and labourers had been pouring concrete, installing guns, laying mine-fields, and peppering North Sea and Atlantic beachs with every king of obstacle — Teller mines, hedgehogs, tetrahedra, 'Belgian gates' and stakes — to strengthen Hitler's 'Atlantic Wall'. Behind this wall of fortifications, running from Norway to the Mediterranean, stood 10 panzer, 17 infantry and 31 training or coast-defence divisions. The equipment, training and morale of the SS and panzer divisions of this force was superb, but many of the infantry formations — and the coast defence divisions even more so — were of poor quality. The Wehrmacht of 1944 was not the Wehrmacht of the years of blitzkrieg and triumph. In 1943 alone, the

Germans had suffered over two million casualties in the bloody battles in Russia and Italy. Replacements for the dead were almost exhausted, and apart from the very young and the too old the ranks of many units were filled with Croatians, Hungarians, Poles, Russians, French, Negroes, Arabs, Turks, Kasaks, and even Indian 'volunteers.'

In the actual invasion area of *Festung Europa* Rommel controlled only three panzer divisions in addition to the four coast-defence divisions manning fortifications, two infantry divisions and the German garrison of Cherbourg. The remainder of his troops were frozen, partly because of the disruptive Allied bombing offensive and partly by Hitler's order. Obsessed by the idea that the Allies would push their assault straight across the Straits of Dover and invade the Pas de Calais area, the Führer insisted that Rommel's troops should remain in the areas allocated to them and that none of the panzer divisions should move

Below: A Sturmgeschütz III Ausf.G rumbles down a French street in 1943. Production of these assault guns started in October 1942. Initially they were organised into 18-gun 'Assault-Gun' battalions each of three batteries of six Sturmgeschütz IIIs. Later these battalions were expanded to become Assault Artillery brigades of up to 45 Sturmgeschütz IIIs. (Three 14 gun batteries and a headquarter section with three other Sturmgeschütz) and a small infantry component. Sturmgeschütz were the artillery's elite, and they had an impressive record of tank kills — 20,000 enemy tanks, it was said by early 1944 alone.

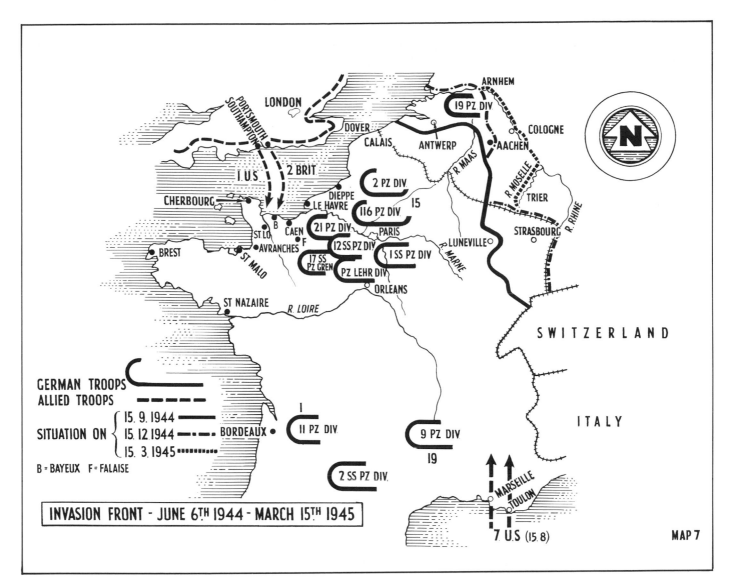

LONDON
PORTSMOUTH
SOUTHAMPTON
DOVER
CALAIS
ARNHEM
19 PZ DIV
COLOGNE
ANTWERP
AACHEN
R. MAAS
R. MOSELLE
TRIER
R. RHINE
1.U.S
2 BRIT
CHERBOURG
DIEPPE
LE HAVRE
2 PZ DIV
116 PZ DIV
15
STRASBOURG
B
CAEN
21 PZ DIV
PARIS
LUNEVILLE
ST LO
F
12 SS PZ DIV
R. MARNE
AVRANCHES
17 SS PZ GREN
1 SS PZ DIV
BREST
ST MALO
PZ LEHR DIV
ORLEANS
ST NAZAIRE
R. LOIRE
SWITZERLAND

GERMAN TROOPS
ALLIED TROOPS

SITUATION ON
{ 15. 9. 1944 ⎯
15. 12. 1944 ⎯·⎯
15. 3. 1945 ·····

ITALY

I
II PZ DIV
BORDEAUX •

9 PZ DIV
19

B = BAYEUX   F = FALAISE

2 SS PZ DIV.

MARSEILLE
TOULON

INVASION FRONT - JUNE 6TH 1944 - MARCH 15TH 1945

7 U.S (15.8)

MAP 7

Left. The *Wespe* (Wasp), a 105mm gun-howitzer on a PzKpfw II chassis, was undoubtedly one of the most important — and one of the most numerous, self-propelled guns of the war. Some 682 PzIIs were converted to Wasps during 1943 and 1944 — mostly by a Polish firm in Warsaw. They saw wide service in the SP artillery battalions of panzer and panzergrenadier divisions. The one above was photographed in France during the winter of 1943/44.

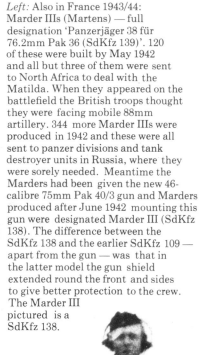

Left: Also in France 1943/44: Marder IIIs (Martens) — full designation 'Panzerjäger 38 für 76.2mm Pak 36 (SdKfz 139)'. 120 of these were built by May 1942 and all but three of them were sent to North Africa to deal with the Matilda. When they appeared on the battlefield the British troops thought they were facing mobile 88mm artillery. 344 more Marder IIIs were produced in 1942 and these were all sent to panzer divisions and tank destroyer units in Russia, where they were sorely needed. Meantime the Marders had been given the new 46-calibre 75mm Pak 40/3 gun and Marders produced after June 1942 mounting this gun were designated Marder III (SdKfz 138). The difference between the SdKfz 138 and the earlier SdKfz 109 — apart from the gun — was that in the latter model the gun shield extended round the front and sides to give better protection to the crew. The Marder III pictured is a SdKfz 138.

without his specific order. The result was that the brunt of the invasion was borne by General Friedrich Dollman's Seventh Army,' and many of the panzers which were immediately available in the Normandy region were frittered away in piecemeal counter-attacks. The remainder resisted stubbornly, falling back across the Normandy *bocage* (checker-board of small fields) as the veterans of two campaigning seasons in Russia demonstrated their professionalism. Rommel had hoped to bring up the whole of his panzer force while the invaders were trying to force a pasage through mine fields, barbed wire and other obstacles on the beaches, and to pour fire on to the foreshore. 'The first twenty-four hours', he averred, 'will be decisive'. But the Führer's fixation that

another Allied assault would come in the Pas de Calais area precluded the execution of Rommel's plan and when the panzers were released they came in dribs and drabs.

By the middle of June however, with the Allies making only slow and costly progress southwards through the *bocage,* the Germans caught their second wind. More of the panzer divisions were released by Hitler and the British trying to seize Caen found they were opposed by no less than six panzer divisions and an AA-Panzergrenadier division. But it was too late. Caen fell, the Americans crunched their way into St Lô, and armoured formations of the US Third Army whirled through the Avranches gap to scour Brittany and then turn south to the Loire. With the US Army pivoting towards Avranches the manoeuvre took on the appearance of one of the classic Panzer encirclements. But then, following a direct order by Hitler, the Germans launched a vicious counter-attack — every available panzer being hurled westwards towards Avranches in an attempt to isolate the US Third Army and, ultimately, to turn north and crush the Normandy beachhead. The attack was eventually halted, and the Americans from the south-west and the British from the north resumed their pincer movement.

In the event the pincers did not close in time to cut off completely what was now left of the German Seventh and the Fifth Panzer Army. 100,000 Germans died and

Below: PzKpfw IV near the 'Invasion Front' in 1944.

Right: PzKpfw IV near the 'Invasion Front' in 1944. Equipped with the L/48 75mm gun, and fitted with the *Schürzen* plates (skirting plates on the side for protection against infantry anti-tank weapons of the bazooka type).

Far right, top: Another PzKpfw IV in France 1944. Like the previous illustrations this Pz IV is fitted with the L/48 gun and is therefore of 1943 vintage or later. Note that skirting plates have not been fitted.

Far right, centre: 'Heidi', a PzKpfw IV of earlier vintage, in France 1944. This has the short 75mm L/24 gun. 'Heidi' has clearly been modified, but she could have fought in the French campaign in 1940.

Far right, bottom: In panzer units — and the Wehrmacht generally — orders tended to be much less formal than in the British and American armies. In this photograph, taken in Normandy in June 1944, a panzergrenadier officer is briefing two of his section leaders. The vehicle is an APC (Schützenpanzer SdKfz 251).

50,000 were taken prisoners in the 'Falaise pocket', moreover most of the divisions which got away were badly mauled. With four Allied armies hard on their heels the disorganized remnants of the *Festung Europa* armies reeled back in full retreat.

The bulk of the panzer divisions escaped and lived to fight another day, but the German position in France was now on the point of collapse. To hasten the disintegration process General Patch's US Seventh Army supported by the French II Corps landed in the south of France on 15 August. This invasion was a 'walk-in' as the Germans had been forced to denude the Riviera coast of all but four second-line divisions, and the subsequent advance inland produced more supply problems than tactical difficulties. Only the action at Montelimar is worthy of note — worthy because it showed that a well-handled panzer division (in this instance the under-strength 11th PD) was still a force to be reckoned with. At Montelimar the panzers held off the American Seventh Army while the rest of the retreating German Nineteenth Army fought its way out of a trap in the Rhone valley.

Paris was liberated on 25 August and by mid-December the German forces — chewed, disrupted and battered — were back behind the ramshackle Siegfied Line, seemingly vulnerable to an Allied coup de grâce. More than half a million Germans had been killed or captured in the Allied drive through France, and on any normal calculation they had absolutely no chance of scraping up reserves to hold their 800km frontier from Switzerland to the North Sea. But German discipline held, the factories continued to turn out armoured vehicles and other war material during an amazing rally which was to prolong the war for another eight months.

The Battle of the Bulge

In mid-November the six Allied armies on the Western Front launched a general offensive which brought only disappointingly small results at heavy cost. A month later the Germans gave the Allies a shock by launching a counter-offensive.

They chose the hilly and wooded country of the Ardennes for the launching of their offensive. Despite what had happened in 1940, this area was generally regarded as difficult country. At the same time the thick woods could conceal the forces concentrating for the attack, while the high ground was very suitable for panzer operations. The chief danger was Allied air-power, and Field Marshal Model summed up the problem as follows: 'Enemy No 1 is the hostile air force which, because of its absolute superiority, tries to destroy our spearheads of attack and our artillery through fighter-bomber attacks and bomb carpets, and to render movement in the rear impossible.' So the operation was launched after a period of fog, rain and snow had blanketed Allied aerial observation and nobbled combat capabilities.

The Germans needed all the advantages they could possibly secure. They were playing for high stakes with limited funds. The striking force comprised the Fifth and Sixth Panzer Armies to which had been given the bulk of the tanks that could be scraped together. The aim of the offensive was to break through to Antwerp, drive a wedge between the British and Americans, isolate the British force, cut its supply lines and then crush it before turning on the Americans. Fifth Panzer Army was to break through the American front in the Ardennes, swerve westwards, then wheel north across the Meuse, past Namur to Antwerp. Sixth Panzer Army, under SS General Sepp Dietrich, was to thrust north-west past Liege to Antwerp.

Complete surprise was achieved, and in the alarm and confusion created on the Allied side the German offensive made considerable progress in the first few days. Near Malmedy, *Kampfgruppe Peiper*, a battle group of the SS Panzer Division under command of Oberst Joachim Peiper, overran an American convoy, and some 86 Americans were massacred; the panzers were on the march, they said, and could not be bothered with prisoners. Behind the US lines, *Einheit Stielau*, a unit of the 150th Panzer Brigade wearing American uniforms, drove around in American jeeps cutting telephone lines, spreading rumours and misdirecting traffic.

For a time the German plan seemed to be going well. But four miles short of the Meuse the offensive was slowed and

stopped. Fuel shortages occasioned by the failure to capture Allied stocks of petrol, the wintry weather and growing Allied air pressure made the end inevitable. Realising that the great gamble had been lost Hitler permitted the Sixth Panzer Army to be withdrawn.

Order for the day published by the commander of a panzergrenadier battalion after learning that six of his men had deserted:

"Traitors from our ranks have deserted to the enemy... These bastards have given away important military secrets... Deceitful Jewish mud-slingers taunt you with their pamphlets and try to entice you into becoming bastards also. Let them spew their poison! We stand watch over Germany's frontier. Death and destruction to all enemies who tread on German soil. As for the contemptible traitors who have forgotten their honour, rest assured the Division will see to it that they never see home and loved ones again. Their families will have to atone for their treason. The destiny of a people has never depended on traitors and bastards. The true German soldier was and is the best in the world. Unwavering behind him is the Fatherland.

And at the end is our Victory.

Long live Germany: Heil the Führer!"

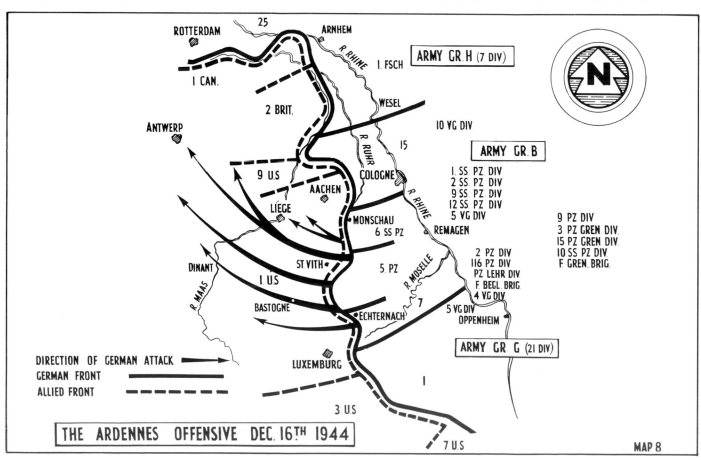

THE ARDENNES OFFENSIVE DEC. 16TH 1944

MAP 8

ARMY GR. H (7 DIV)

ARMY GR. B
1. SS. PZ. DIV.
2 SS. PZ. DIV.
9 SS. PZ. DIV.
12 SS. PZ. DIV.
5 VG DIV

9 PZ DIV
3 PZ GREN. DIV.
15 PZ GREN. DIV.
10 SS PZ. DIV.
F. GREN. BRIG.

2 PZ DIV
116 PZ DIV
PZ LEHR DIV.
F. BEGL. BRIG.
4 VG DIV

5 VG DIV
OPPENHEIM

ARMY GR. G (21 DIV)

10 VG DIV

6 SS PZ
5. PZ
7

DIRECTION OF GERMAN ATTACK →
GERMAN FRONT ——
ALLIED FRONT - - -

ROTTERDAM 25 ARNHEM
I. FSCH
1 CAN.
2 BRIT.
WESEL
ANTWERP
COLOGNE
9 US
AACHEN
LIÉGE
MONSCHAU
REMAGEN
DINANT
ST VITH
1 US
BASTOGNE
ECHTERNACH
LUXEMBURG
3 US
7 US
R. RHINE
R. RUHR
R. RHINE
R. MOSELLE
R. MAAS

Leutnant Michael Wittmann of the 501st Panzer Battalion earned a Knight's Cross with 'Tigers'. In Russia he was credited with 119 T-34s before his unit was transferred to France. Soon after the Allied invasion Wittmann's battalion was moved from Beauvais to Normandy, with orders to stop the British 7th Armoured Division taking Caen. On 13 June Wittmann, with only five operational Tigers took up a position in a wood on some high ground near the village of Villers Bocage.

Wittmann's Tiger was the first to open the engagement when it fired at the half-track leading an armoured column of British vehicles towards Villers Bocage. A direct hit was registered and with the half-track blocking the road in front Wittmann turned his attention to the last vehicle. When this went up in flames Wittmann knocked out the rest of the British vehicles, one by one. In about five minutes Wittmann's 88mm gun and two machine guns destroyed 25 vehicles, while his four other Tigers were dealing with a squadron of Cromwell tanks. At dusk the Germans were occupying Villers Bocage, and although they lost six Tigers in the course of the day 25 British tanks, 14 half-tracks, 14 carriers had been destroyed and the invaders had suffered over a hundred casualties.

The story was the same throughout this period of the campaign: the kill-loss ratio of the Tigers was very much in their favour.

In another action near Caen Tigers of No 3 Abteilung 503 Panzer Battalion were pitted against 20 Shermans. 13 Shermans were knocked out and two captured without loss or casualties on the German side. Six days later when the British attempted to break out of the area east of Caen six Tigers meted out heavy punishment on the flank of the British advance. And even during the fighting for the Falaise Pocket the Tigers continued to live up to their reputation — just two Tigers being able to hold up the whole spearhead of the 53rd Infantry Division.

The Russian Counter-Offensive.

The year 1942 did not bring Hitler the victory he had expected in Russia. Indeed, by the end of the year the German armies had been compelled to withdraw along the whole front. Subsequently, the annihilation of the German Sixth Army and the destruction of the Rumanian, Italian and Hungarian Armies in Russia was to mark another year of crises, improvisation and reverses. In every theatre of war the story was the same. In Africa the campaign ended with the surrender of what was left of the

Top left: Panthers on the 'Invasion Front'; in the summer of 1944.

Centre left: Panthers played a prominent part in the large-scale defensive battles in Normandy, where mobility was less important than their frontal protection and the formidable (935 m/s) gun that could penetrate 120mm of 30 degree armour plate at 900 metres. Only crushing Allied air power and numerical superiority on the ground prevented this technological advantage becoming decisive strategically.

Below left: PzKpfw IV and PzKpfw VI Tiger of the 1st SS Pz Corps *Leibstandarte* Division. Falaise 1944. When the Germans launched their offensive in the Ardennes in the winter of 1944 only 100 Tiger IIs were available. However they soon made their presence felt. The mere appearance of these ponderous tanks was to result in the evacuation of St Vith. Even in retreat, under air attack and running out of fuel, the Tigers were able to command respect dug in to static positions. At Bastogne on Christmas Eve 1944 Tiger tanks mounted an attack, running amok within the perimeter of the 101st US Airborne Division. One of the last Tiger engagements of any strength was fought along the Berlin-Küstrin road, when 28 Tigers and 27 Panthers withstood 90 minutes of Russian bombardment followed with an attack by a Soviet tank division. Sixty T 34s were turned into blazing wrecks by the time the battle was over, and the Panzers still held their positions.

Deutsche Afrika Korps, and the Allies invaded Italy. In Russia the Germans were forced to give up large tracts of the territory they had overrun in order to avoid an encirclement on a grander scale than Stalingrad. By the middle of February the Russians had battered a 300km gap in the front north of Kharkov, and were advancing west and south-west towards the lower Dnieper and the Sea of Azov. As this threatened to cut off the whole of the German Army Group Don, its commander von Manstein decided to pull back and disengage the First and Fourth Panzer Armies and to launch them in an attack on the flank of the advancing Russians.

In sanctioning von Manstein's operation Hitler stipulated that Kharkov must be held at all costs; defending the city at this time was General Paul Hausser's SS–Panzer Corps (which included the elite SS *Leibstandarte Adolf Hitler, Das Reich,* and *Totenkopf* Panzer

Divisions, and the *Grossdeutschland* Panzergrenadier Division). In defiance of Hitler's order to stand fast and hold the ground his troops were occupying, Hausser decided on his own account to sally forth in a sorties against the advancing Russians. (What happened then is not important in itself, except as part of von Manstein's bigger operation. But Hausser's action tends to refute the generally accepted view that all SS units were Hitler's private army, officered by fanatical individuals who believed only in blind obedience to the Führer. In fact the Waffen-SS divisions were top-class fighting formations, and the majority of their officers behaved in accordance with tactical requirements and not as party representatives. Due to the fact that the Waffen-SS, and formations like the *Grossdeutschland* Division were given the very best weapons, equipment and personnel their classification as elite units often led to misinterpretations. In the

event the crack SS units retained their esprit de corps to the end, and when Germany finally capitulated they destroyed their equipment and then marched proudly in to surrender — at a time when other units were slouching into captivity.)

Von Manstein now launched his offensive, employing large numbers of the new Tigers (Panzer VI) for the first time. By the middle of March despite the odds of seven to one, he had halted the Russian drive, secured Kharkov, and straightened out the German front. It was a remarkable achievement — one of the greatest military feats of the war.

Even Hitler had now come to realize that the Germans could not launch another major offensive in Russia and for three or four weeks after the battles around Kharkov there was a lull in the fighting. The winter snows were now

thawing, vehicles moving on the unsurfaced roads quickly turned them into rutted and impassable mud paths. By the middle of April however, with the winter improving and the roads drying out, Hitler gave orders for the execution of Operation Citadel — a limited assault against the Russian salient west of Kursk. The operation was intended to regain the initiative before the Allies landed in Italy and before they could open yet another 'Front' in Europe.

Operation Citadel

Nineteen panzer divisions — nearly all the panzers stationed in the east — were concentrated for the operation and at Hitler's insistence Panthers (Panzer V) were to participate. In the event, because of production problems in the factories producing the Panthers, the Führer's insistence on employing Panthers caused

Below: The ubiquitous PzKpfw III still in service in mid-1943 although production of this tank was to terminate in August. (In this photograph an infantry casualty is being ferried back to a medical aid post.)

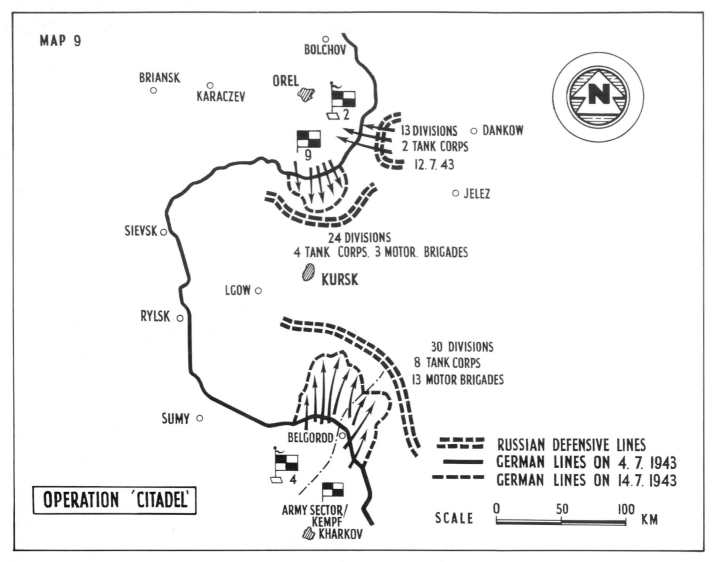

MAP 9

BRIANSK

KARACZEV

BOLCHOV

OREL

2

9

13 DIVISIONS
2 TANK CORPS
12. 7. 43

DANKOW

JELEZ

SIEVSK

24 DIVISIONS
4 TANK CORPS. 3 MOTOR. BRIGADES

KURSK

LGOW

RYLSK

30 DIVISIONS
8 TANK CORPS
13 MOTOR BRIGADES

SUMY

BELGOROD

4

RUSSIAN DEFENSIVE LINES
GERMAN LINES ON 4. 7. 1943
GERMAN LINES ON 14. 7. 1943

OPERATION 'CITADEL'

ARMY SECTOR/
KEMPF
KHARKOV

SCALE   0   50   100   KM

Left: The Panther Panzer V (PzKpfw V) was undoubtedly the most advanced tank design of its time, but Hitler's insistence on its participation in Operation Citadel was a bad start. The operation failed because it had to be postponed until the Panthers were ready, and teething troubles in the fuel system were extra hazards for their crews. It was several months before these and other production difficulties were overcome. As originally planned the weight and dimensions of the Panther were the counterpart of the Soviet T-34.

the date of the operation to be postponed several times. By the time the final date had been set as 4 July the Russians knew the German plans, and they had made their preparations.

The Russians opposed the German forces with 54 infantry divisions, 12 armoured corps and 16 mechanised brigades (a disparity of about 3:1). The Germans had only 600 fewer tanks than at the beginning of the Russian campaign, but since 1941 the firepower of tanks had increased considerably on both sides. With 1,800 combat aircraft of the Luftwaffe — the same number as was available in 1941 — the Germans had never previously assembled such a powerful military force. Photographs of the time showing the great concentration of German material convey a false impression of German strength, the same impression which produced an unjustified optimism among the German troops in the battle zone. But conditions had changed in the two years that had elapsed since the start of Operation Barbarossa. The Russian commanders had gained confidence, morale in the Red Army was high and training methods had improved. When the Panzers attacked they came up against an enemy, in well prepared positions, who was expecting them.

Following dive-bombing and artillery bombardments the assault began as planned at 1500hrs on 4 July, and ran into difficulties almost immediately. Mines and other obstacles made the creation of a gap in the Russian lines more difficult than had been anticipated, and determined and clearly well-rehearsed counter-attacks proved that the German assault had been anticipated. The Panther failed to come up to expectations, while an intensified and skilful Russian anti-tank defence brought fierce tank battles and heavy losses with virtually nothing to show for them. In the north, the German Ninth Army was back on its start-line positions after a week of heavy fighting, and although the Fourth Panzer Army managed a 35km advance it had failed to open a gap in the Russian line, and the jaws of the projected pincer were still 100km apart. On 12 July the Ninth Army had to break off the attack in order to fight off a massive counter-attack on their rear at Orel. 'Citadel' was turning into a disaster for the Germans, and when Hitler ordered all operations round Kursk to be called off the German had suffered irreparable losses — including 3,000 tanks and 5,000 other vehicles. The battles of Operation Citadel marked the

end of the massed German panzer assaults in the East. Hitler's growing concern was with what was happening in the West and he began to withdraw panzer divisions from the Eastern front.

By 1944 the panzers were already exhausted; units and individuals of panzer and panzergrenadier divisions would fight on to the bitter end. But the heady days of the true panzer war were over.

Winter 1944
During the German retreat through Poland to East Prussia the Baltic port of Klaipeda (Memel) became a German Dunkirk from which many thousands of refugees as well as troops were evacuated. Remnants of the *Grossdeutschland* Panzergrenadier Division were among the units which defended the perimeter of the port:
'Memel was ringed with innumerable carcasses of Russian tanks, and there were as many anti-tank gunners as there were ordinary soldiers. Carloads of mines were driven out by civilian volunteers and

Above: Tiger of the *Leibstandarte 1st SS-Panzer Division.* Adolf Hitler stated in 1944 that: 'One battalion of Tigers is worth a normal Panzer Division . . .'

Above: Panther Panzer V
(PzKpfw V).

Right: Tiger I.

placed in front of our defences by the infantry in the course of small counter-attacks organised solely for this manoeuvre. We were defenceless only against the Russian fighter-bombers which flew over continually. To the northwest of our position the remains of several dismantled railway carriages underwent eight attacks in two days. What was left of our anti-aircraft defence was concentrated around the piers, where the peril was greatest. This target constituted a real danger to the Russian pilots, who preferred to attack the rest of the stronghold, where there was no serious resistance.

Anyway, I remember that one grey afternoon, some elements of our division were regrouped at a certain spot. Ammunition was handed out, and we were given two tins of food each, without regard to the contents. Some received a pound of apple sauce, others a pound of margarine. However, these variations seemed insignificant compared to the fact that the ghost of German military organisation was still functioning during those days of grace on the fringes of a

disintegrated city, which would still be known as Memel for a short time. Supplies, although obviously rationed to the limit, were still distributed before an offensive. Incredible as it may now seem, the vestigial remnants of the German Army in Memel were to attempt an offensive to the south, whose aim was to re-establish contact with the front at Cranz and Königsberg. To most of us old soldiers, the idea was absurd. A few tanks which were still intact were to support our progress. Material which belonged to the Kurland soldiers, and even some from Germany, had been delivered. We were to proceed to a village some ten miles to the south, on the road which followed the coast, beside a large bay. The commanding officer of the operation chose a moment of appalling weather to launch his offensive. It was simultaneously snowing and raining. The atmospheric conditions were so disastrous that even the Russian artillery had practically stopped functioning. It was this circumstance which our leaders hoped to exploit on our last, lunatic expedition.

A dozen dirty-grey tanks went out to

Above: Servicing a PzKpfw V Panther in a rear rally.

Above: PzKpfw IV Russia 1944. Many of the panzers had travelled many miles and losing a track was a common occurrence.

meet an inexorable fate. The black crosses painted on their sides, the colour of our misery, were scarcely visible. Inside the turrets, the 'Ride of the Valkyries' was coming over the short-wave radios — a fitting accompaniment to supreme sacrifice. Decrepit trucks carrying field pieces and heavy machine guns followed close behind, replacing the full-track caissons of panzergrenadiers of our prosperous days. A mass of infantry, mixed with the remnants of naval and aerial groups, ran along beside the motorised column. My group clung to the exposed chassis of an automobile which had been stripped of its skin.

Anyway, our point units surprised a camp of Russian armour lined up under the snow as if on parade. The Russians staggered by this absolutely unforeseen blow, abandoned the camp, which we burned, using one of our special incendiary techniques. A supply of Soviet fuel allowed us to think of pushing our offensive even farther, and we went on, despite the gusts of wind which lashed us. Several concentrations of Russian troops gave way when they saw us coming.

However, the enemy was massed around Memel in depth, and as soon as they struck back, our offensive came to an end. We could hear the first Russian reaction, and knew that we would soon be inundated by a merciless rain of fire, and that the first Russian tanks were already rolling toward us.

As things were reaching a critical point for us, we heard artillery fire from the sea. The bad weather prevented us from seeing the ships just off shore, but their fire fell on the Red tide as it moved toward us. Two or three destroyers or torpedo boats had come especially to support us. Despite zero visibility, the coordinates supplied by our tanks in forward positions enabled the ships to fire with considerable precision and the Russian thrust was more or less stopped. It was also possible that the Russians, who were further inland, misjudged the source of our fire, and supposed that we possessed more ground artillery than we actually did.

However, none of this made any real difference. The Russians possessed infinitely greater means than we did. Toward the end of the day, our meagre operation was attacked along a flank of some six miles. This was much more than we could take. Soon half our tanks were on fire. As foreseen, we had failed and were ordered to return to Memel — six miles back the way we had come — which was far more difficult than the way out.

We abandoned the road we had followed for our last attack — except for our trucks and the remaining tanks, which separated as widely as possible when the Russians fired. In the darkness, striped with tracer, breathless troops were running across the dunes from one hole to the next, valuing each step which brought them closer to Memel. As a crowning blow, the column had to cross a stretch of road we ourselves had mined that morning. . . . '

The End in Berlin

Gerhard Zilch a former NCO of the 3rd Heavy Flak Battery has given a characteristic picture of the atmosphere among German units in Berlin during the last few days before the city was overran by the Russians. The panzers were finished although Hitler maintained almost to the end that a relief force with Tiger IIs was on its way to the besieged capital of the Third Reich. Without their tanks the Panzers, together with troops from every other corps and arm of the Wehrmacht, were reduced to the role of infantrymen.

'. . . Our leader was SS-Oberstürmfuhrer Babick, battle commandant of the Reichstag. I was acting as runner between the AA gunners and the SS battle group, a part of the Nordland SS Division. [The SS *Freiwillige* Panzergrenadier Division.] Its headquarters were in Europa House near the Anhalter Railway Station . . . Babick was hoping for reinforcements. From somewhere or other, marines had come to Berlin on the night of 28 April, led by a Lieutenant-Commander who was now hanging about the cellar with nothing to say for himself. Babick never moved from his map, plotting the areas from which he expected

Below left and right:
Sturmgeschütz III Ausf.G 'somewhere in South Russia' 1943. These photographs show the limited traverse available for the 75mm gun. By 1944 many of the assault guns had added an anti-aircraft machine gun to their armament as an extra defensive measure.

Left and below: Hummel — medium self-propelled 150mm gun-howitzer on a PzKpfw IV chassis — in action near Kharkov in 1943. 105mm assault howitzer on a PzKpfw III chassis.

reinforcements and even the arrival of "Royal Tigers".

Babick was still bubbling over with confidence. For one thing, he thought himself perfectly safe in his shelter. SS sentries were posted outside, others barred the corridor to the Reichstag, and Royal Tigers, our finest weapons, were apparently just round the corner. He had divided his men into groups of five to ten. One group was commanded by SS Unterstürmfuhrer Undermann (or something like that; I didn't get the name quite clearly); he was posted south of the Moltke bridge in the Ministry of the Interior (the building the Russians called 'Himmler's House') and the bridge itself lay in his line of fire.

Then an SS subaltern, aged about nineteen, came to Babick with the report that Undermann and his men had come across some alcohol and that they had got roaring drunk. As a precaution he had brought Undermann along; he was waiting outside. Babick roared out the order: 'Have him shot on the spot'. The subaltern clicked his heels and run out. Seconds later we heard a burst of fire from a sub-machine gun. The boy reappeared and reported: 'Orders carried out.' Babick put him in charge of Undermann's unit.

Our ranks in the Reichstag got thinner and thinner and by the night of 30 April, no more than forty to fifty people, soldiers and civilians, were left in the cellar. This remnant was now busy lookig for the safest possible hiding-places. There we intended to sit tight until the Russians came. But they kept us waiting for another twenty-four hours. At dawn on 1 May, we heared over our portable radio that the Führer had 'fallen in the battle for the Reich Capital', his wife at his side. Goebbels and his family had gone the same way. We were our own masters, at long last . . .'

The Panzer Divisions

Most of the armoured, panzergrenadier, and motorised infantry divisions were regular formations. Some other ad hoc formations were constituted for particular operations and then disbanded. The major units shown in each division are those which were on the establishment in 1944. Before then some of the units were with other formations — 15th Panzer Regiment, for example, started out in 1938 as the armoured regiment of the 5th Panzer Division, but was subsequently transferred to the 11th Panzer Division when the latter was raised in October 1940.

Divisional signs existed only after October 1940 when the German High Command decreed that the eighteen panzer divisions then in existence should display allotted symbols. Subsequently in 1941 every German division adopted a sign, and — unlike the original symbols — these signs were designed to reflect the traditions of the individual divisions. The signs were painted on the division's vehicles: infantry divisions in white, panzer divisions in yellow, mountain divisions in green — either direct on the dark basic grey colouring of the vehicles or on a small black shield. Some divisions were called after their signs: the 11th Panzer, for example being known as the 'Ghost Division' on account of its spectral emblem — a skeleton riding on the tracks of a tank brandishing a sword.

On occasions divisional signs were changed as a deceptive measure. In May 1942, for instance, the 6th Panzer Regiment, whose correct divisional flash was the double cross illustrated here, was withdrawn from the fighting around Leningrad. Having been re-equipped and made up to strength it returned to Russia in December with its vehicles displaying a new sign — an axe on a black background.

1st Panzer
Formed October 1935 at Weimer; based IXth Military District Kassel.

Major Units:
Panzergrenadier Regiments 1, 113
Panzer Regiment 1
Panzer Artillery Regiment 73
Panzer Aufkl Abt (Recce Section) 1.

Campaigns:
Poland 1939; Belgium and France 1940; North and Central Russia June 1941-Feb 1943; Balkans and Greece 1943; Ukraine Nov-Dec 1943; Hungary and Austria June 1944-May 1945.

2nd Panzer
Formed October 1935 at Würzburg; based XVII Military District Vienna.

Major Units:
Panzergrenadier Regiments 2, 304
Panzer Regiment 3
Panzer Artillery Regiment 74
Panzer Aufkl Abt (Recce) 2

Campaigns:
Poland 1939; France 1940; Balkans and Greece 1941; Central Russia (Smolensk, Orel, Kiev) 1942-1943; France and Germany 1944-45.

3rd Panzer
Formed October 1935 at Berlin; based III Military District Berlin.

Major Units:
Panzergrenadier Regiments 3, 394
(Pzgdr Regiment No 3 was originally a motor-cycle bn.)
Panzer Regiment 6
Panzer Artillery Regiment 75
Panzer Aufkl Abt 3

Campaigns:
Poland 1939, France 1940; Central Russia 1941-1942, Southern Russia (Kharkov, Dnepr Bend) 1943; Ukraine and Poland 1944; Hungary and Austria 1944-1945.

4th Panzer
Formed November 1938 at Würzburg; based XIII Military District Nuremberg

Major Units:
Panzergrenadier Regiments 12, 33
Panzer Regiment 35
Panzer Artillery Regiment 103
Panzer Aufkl Abt 4

Campaigns:
Poland 1939; France 1940; Central Russia 1941-1944 (Caucasus 1942, Kursk 1943, Latvia 1944); Germany 1945.

1st Panzer

7th Panzer

13th Panzer

19th Panzer

2nd Panzer

8th Panzer

14th Panzer

20th Panzer

3rd Panzer

9th Panzer

15th Panzer

21st Panzer

4th Panzer

10th Panzer

16th Panzer

22nd Panzer

5th Panzer

11th Panzer

17th Panzer

23rd Panzer

6th Panzer

12th Panzer

18th Panzer

24th Panzer

5th Panzer
Formed at Oppeln in November 1939; based VIII Military District Breslau.
Major Units:
Panzergrenadier Regiments 13,14
Panzer Regiment 31
Panzer Artillery Regiment 116
Panzer Aufkl Abt 5
Campaigns:
France 1941; Yugoslavia and Greece 1941; Central Russia 1941-1944 (Kursk, Dnepr, Latvia, Kurland) East Prussia 1944-45.

6th Panzer
Formed at Wuppertal in October 1939 from the Wehrmacht's 1st Light Division; based on VI Military District Münster.
Major Units:
Panzergrenadier Regiments 4, 114
Panzer Regiment 11
Panzer Artillery Regiment 76
Panzer Aufkl Abt 6
Campaigns:
France 1944; Russia 1941-44 — with a brief spell for re-fitting in France in 1942; Hungary and Austria 1944-45.

7th Panzer
Formed at Weimar in October 1939 from the 2nd Light Division; based IX Military District Kassel.
Major Units:
Panzergrenadier Regiments 6, 7
Panzer Regiment 25
Panzer Artillery Regiment 78
Panzer Aufkl Abt 7
Campaigns:
France 1940 (under command of Major-General Rommel); Central Russia 1941-42 (refit in France in 1942 and occupation of Vichy); Southern Russia (mainly in the Kharkov region during 1942) 1942-1944; Baltic Coast and Prussia 1944-45.

8th Panzer
Formed at Berlin in October 1939 from the 3rd Light Division; based on III Military District Berlin.
Major Units:
Panzergrenadier Regiments 8, 28
Panzer Regiment 10
Panzer Artillery Regiment 80
Panzer Aufkl Abt 8
Campaigns:
France 1940; Yugoslavia (saw no action) 1941; Northern Russia 1941-1943 (Leningrad, Kholm, Orel, Kiev) Southern Russia 1943-44; Hungary and Yugoslavia 1944-45.

9th Panzer
Formed at Würzburg in August 1940 from 4th Light Division; based XVII Military District Vienna.
Major Units:
Panzergrenadier Regiments 10, 11
Panzer Regiment 33*
Panzer Artillery Regiment 102
Panzer Aufkl Abt 9

Campaigns:
Netherlands and France 1940 and then transferred to Poland; Balkans 1941; Russia 1941-44 (Southern sector 1941, central sector 1942, Kursk 1943); reformed and re-equipped France in 1944 prior to the Normandy campaign (Ardennes offensive 1944-45).
* 33 Panzer Regiment was raised from the Austrian Army Tank Battalion and took the title 'Prinz Eugen Regiment'.

10th Panzer
Formed in April 1939 at Stuttgart; based on V Military District Stuttgart.
Major Units:
Panzergrenadier Regiments 69, 86
Panzer Regiment 7
Panzer Artillery Regiment 90
Panzer Aufkl Abt 10
Campaigns:
Poland 1939; France 1940; Central Russia 1941-1942 (transferred to France for rest and refitting in April 1942, and saw action against the British and Canadians at Dieppe in August that year); Tunisia 1943, where the Division was destroyed.

11th Panzer
Formed in August 1940 from the 11th Rifle Brigade at Breslau; based VIII Military District Breslau.
Major Units:
Panzergrenadier Regiments 110, 111
Panzer Regiment 15
Panzer Artillery Regiment 119
Panzer Aufkl Abt 11
Campaigns:
Balkans 1941; Russia 1941-44 (Orel/Belgorod offensive at Krivoi Rog Area 1943, Korsun Pocket January—May 1944); NW Europe 1944/45 (saw considerable action and suffered heavy casualties during the Allied landings in Normandy).

12th Panzer
Formed in October 1940 from the 2nd Motorised Infantry Division; based on the II Military District at Stettin.
Major Units:
Panzergrenadier Regiments 5, 25
Panzer Regiment 29
Panzer Artillery Regiment 2
Panzer Aufkl Abt 12
Campaigns:
Russia 1941-1944 (Central sector between Minsk and Smolensk in 1941, siege of Leningrad 1942, Orel and Middle Dnepr 1943. Captured by the Red Army in Kurland sector early in 1945).

13th Panzer
Formed in October 1940 from the 13th Motorised Infantry Division; based on XI Military District Hannover.
Major Units:
Panzergrenadier Regiments 66, 93
Panzer Regiment 4

Panzer Artillery Regiment 13
Panzer Aufkl Abt 13
Campaigns:
(Until June 1941 this division was stationed in Rumania and employed as a training formation). Russia 1941-1944 (Kiev 1942, Caucasus and the Kuban 1943-44, Krivoi Rog area 1944; returned to Germany to refit in September 1944); Hungary 1944-45. (During the German defence of Budapest the division was virtually annihilated, but it was subsequently reformed as the Panzer Grenadier Division *Feldherrenhalle 2*.

14th Panzer
Formed in August 1940 from the 4th Infantry Division; based on IV Military District Dresden.
Major Units:
Panzergrenadier Regiments 103, 108
Panzer Regiment 36
Panzer Artillery Regiment 4
Panzer Aufkl Abt 14
Campaigns:
Yugoslavia 1941 (stationed in Germany until February 1941, moved to Hungary in March of that year and then, the following month to Yugoslavia); Southern Russia July 1941 — December 1942 (Encircled in Stalingrad and wiped out. Division reformed in Brittany in October 1943 and returned to Russia the following month). Russia 1943-1945 (Dnepr Bend, Ukraine, Kurland).

15th Panzer
Formed in August 1940 from the 33rd Infantry Division and shipped to North Africa in February 1941 as part of the original Deutsches Afrika Korps.
Major Units:
(during its existence as a Panzer Division)
Panzergrenadier Regiments 104, 115
Panzer Regiment 8
Panzer Artillery Regiment 33
Panzer Aufkl Abt 15
Campaigns':
The 15th Panzer was continuously engaged in North Africa from February 1941 until May 1943 when the German forces in that theatre surrendered in Tunisia. In July 1943 it was reformed in Sicly as the 15th Panzergrenadier Division.

16th Panzer
Formed in August 1940 and based on the VIth Military District Münster.
Major Units:
Panzergrenadier Regiments 64, 79
Panzer Regiment 2
Panzer Artillery Regiment 16
Panzer Aufkl Abt 16
Campaigns:
Southern Russia June 1941 — December 1942 Annihilated at Stalingrad in December '42. Reformed in France in March 1943 and moved to Italy (Taranto region) in June that year. (Opposed Allied landings at Salerno and subsequently engaged in the Naples area). Transferred to Russia in November 1943. Russia 1943-45. (Suffered heavy casualties around Kiev in November 1943).

17th Panzer
Formed in October 1940 and based on the VIIth Military District, Munich.
Major Units:
Panzergrenadier Regiments 40,63
Panzer Regiment 39
Panzer Artillery Regiment 27
Panzer Aufkl Abt 17
Campaigns:
Russia 1941-1945. (Participated in all the major actions in the Central and Southern sectors and during the German retreat across the northern Ukraine.)

18th Panzer
Formed in October 1940 and based on the IVth Military District Dresden.
Major Units:
Panzergrenadier Regiments 52, 101
Panzer Regiment 18
Panzer Artillery Regiment 88
Panzer Aufkl Abt 8
Campaigns:
Russia 1941-1943 (Central and Southern sectors). After suffering heavy casualties around Kiev in October 1943 the division was disbanded and reformed as 18 Artillerie Division.

19th Panzer
Formed in October 1940 and based on the XIth Military District, Hannover.
Major Units:
Panzergrenadier Regiments 73, 74
Panzer Regiment 27
Panzer Artillery Regiment 19
Panzer Aufkl Abt 19
Campaigns:
Russia 1941-44 (Central and Southern sectors). Transferred to East Prussia in July 1944 after suffering heavy casualties when the Germans withdrew across northern Ukraine. Subsequently saw further action near Breslau prior to moving south to Bohemia.

20th Panzer
Formed in October 1940 and based first on the IXth Military District Kassel and later on the XIth District at Hannover.
Major Units:
Panzergrenadier Regiments 59, 112
Panzer Regiment 21
Panzer Artillery Regiment 92
Panzer Aufkl Abt 20
Campaigns:
Russia 1941-1944 (Took part in the offensive to capture Moscow in 1941; subsequently in the Orel offensive in July

1943 and suffered heavy losses in the Soviet summer offensive of 1944). Transferred to Rumania in August 1944; moved to East Prussia in November 1944, and to Hungary in December that year.

21st Panzer
Formed 'in the field' during February 1941, from the 5th Light Motorised Division, Panzer Regiment 5 and cadres from the 3rd Panzer Division.

Major Units:
Panzergrenadier Regiments 125, 192
Panzer Regiment 22
Panzer Artillery Regiment 155
Panzer Aufkl Abt 21
Campaigns:
This famous division, the second major component of the Deutsche Afrika Korps, served continuously in the desert campaigns from February 1941 until it was over-run in Tunisia in May 1943. It was badly mauled at Alam Halfa and suffered heavy casualties at El Alamein.

In July 1943 it was reformed in Normandy, serving as a training formation until June 1944 when it was heavily engaged in Normandy. Subsequently it saw further action in the Saar and Alsace areas before being transferred to the Eastern Front and being over-run by the Red Army in the final weeks of the war.

22nd Panzer
Formed in October 1941 in France, and based on the XIIth Military District, Wiesbàden.

Major Units:
Panzergrenadier Regiments 129, 140
Panzer Regiment 204
Panzer Artillery Regiment 140
Panzer Aufkl Abt 140
Campaigns:
This division was sent to the central sector of the Russian front in March 1942, and was virtually wiped out in the fighting around Stalingrad in December. Although the remnants of some units survived the division was disbanded. Only Panzergrenadier Regiment 129 retained its identity and this unit was transferred to the 15th Panzergrenadier Division.

23rd Panzers
Formed in October 1941 in France and based on the XIIth Military District Stuttgart.

Major Units:
Panzergrenadier Regiments 126, 128
Panzer Regiment 23
Panzer Artillery Regiment 128
Panzer Aufkl Abt 23.
Campaigns:
Russia 1942-1944. (Kharkov and the Caucasus, and Stalingrad 1943 — where it managed to escape encirclement;

Dnepr Bend February 1944. Refitted in Poland in the summer of 1944 and moved to Hungary.)

24th Panzer
Formed in February 1942 from the 1st Cavalry Division and based on Military District I at Königsberg.

Major Units:
Panzergrenadier Regiments 21, 26
Panzer Regiment 24
Panzer Artillery Regiment 89
Panzer Aufkl Abt 24
Campaigns:
Following the re-organisation, re-equipping and conversion of the 1st Cavalry Division into a panzer division, the 24th Pz Division was sent to the southern sector of the Russian front. Having been wiped out at Stalingrad between December 1942 and January 1943, it was reformed in March 1943 in Normandy and sent to northern Italy. In October 1943 however, it returned to the Russian front where it again suffered heavy casualties. (Kiev and Dnepr Bend). Subsequently it saw further action in Poland during the Soviet summer offensive of 1944, in Hungary and Slovakia (1944-45) before it withdrew to Schleswig-Holstein prior to surrendering to the British in May 1945.

25th Panzer
Formed in February 1942 from units of the occupation forces in Norway, and based on the VIth Military District at Münster.

Major Units:
Panzergrenadier Regiments 146, 147
Panzer Regiment 9
Panzer Artillery Regiment 91
Panzer Aufkl Abt 25
Campaigns:
Following its transfer to the south of France in August 1943, this division was moved to the southern sector of the Russian front in October 1943. There it saw action before Kiev, and took part in the withdrawal from northern Ukraine in March 1944. The following month it was pulled back to Denmark to refit, returning to the central sector of the Eastern Front in September. It then fought on the Vistula line and in defence of Warsaw prior to withdrawing to Germany in February 1945 and being over-run by the Red Army in May.

26th Panzer
Formed in Brittany during October 1942, from the 23rd Infantry Division, and based on the IIIrd Military District, Berlin.

Major Units:
Panzergrenadier Regiments 9, 67
Panzer Regiment 26
Panzer Artillery Regiment 93

Panzer Aufkl Abt 26

Campaigns:

This division moved to Italy in July 1943 and served there throughout the rest of the war, being heavily and constantly engaged between the Apennines and the Adriatic coast in November 1944.

27th Panzer

This division existed in embryo form for less than six months. While it was being formed in France in 1942 the headquarters and those units which had been allotted to it were ordered up to the Russian front, and heavy casualties led to its disbandment early in 1943.

116th Panzer

Formed in France during April 1944 from the 16th Panzer Grenadier Division, and based on the VIth Military District, Münster.

Major Units:

Panzergrenadier Regiments 60, 156

Panzer Regiment 16

Panzer Artillery Regiment 146

Panzer Aufkl Abt 116.

Campaigns:

This division was continuously engaged in NW Europe from July 1944 until the end of the war. In the Ardennes offensive it suffered heavy casualties, and again in the Kleve area in January 1945.

The Panzer - Lehr Division

The renowned Panzer-Lehr Division was formed in France during 1944 by amalgamating demonstration units and training formations attached to the various German armoured warfare schools. Initially it was commanded by General-Major Fritz Bayerlein, Rommel's old chief-of-staff, and apart from its unusually able and experienced personnel it had twice the normal complement of armour. (With 190 tanks, 40 self-propelled guns and 612 talf-tracks it was the Wehrmacht's most powerful panzer division in June 1944)

Major Units:

Panzergrenadier Regiments 901, 902

Panzer Lehr Regiment 103

Panzer Artillery Lehr Regiment 130

Panzer Aufkl Lehr Rgt Abt 130

Campaigns:

The Panzer-Lehr Division was heavily engaged in the fighting in NW Europe — from Normandy to the Ruhr. In the Normandy fighting it suffered abnormally heavy casualties but it was re-equipped and re-inforced for the Ardennes offensive.

Other Panzer formations

Panzergrenadier Divisions are listed on page 136 and SS-Panzer Divisions on page 144.

Of the panzergrenadier divisions the most famous, the *Grossdeutschland Division* deserves special mention. This élite formation evolved originally from the Berlin Watch Regiment. By 1940, when it fought in France under command of General Graf von Schwerin, it was a motorised infantry regiment, but two years later it had expanded into a panzergrenadier division. Finally because its armoured strength matched that of a panzer division it could be considered more of a panzer than a panzergrenadier formation.

Several other panzer formations were raised in the course of the war. Most of them existed only on paper — being brought into existence as a result of decrees issued by Hitler's headquarters towards the end of the war when many units were no more than flags on the Führer's maps. (Panzer divisions, which were supposed to be raised from the personnel of various schools, reserve organisations etc were given names like *Clausewitz, Holstein, Müncheberg, Donau, Schlesien* and *Westfalen.)*

Feldherrnhalle 2 Division

Formed at the beginning of 1945 from surviving elements of 13th Panzergrenadier Division and the 60th Panzergrenadier Division (originally the 60th Motorised Infantry Division) deserves mention as does the *Panzer Division Kurland.* The former fought in Hungary and Austria until the end of the war, while the Kurland, which was formed about the same time as the Feldherrnhalle from the 14th Panzer Division and other encircled units in the Kurland region also fought on to the bitter end.

Note on the Panzer Reconnaissance Units (Panzeraufklärungs-Abteilung) (Panzer Aufkl Abt.)

Every panzer division had an armoured reconnaissance unit. This was a most effective self-contained battle group equipped with heavy or light armoured cars and two or three motorised infantry companies, with self-propelled field and anti-tank artillery and a platoon of engineers. Half-tracks sometimes took the place of the light armoured cars and the infantry were transported either in half-tracks, Volkswagen trucks or on motor-cycles.

The Panzergrenadier and Motorised Infantry Divisions.

Panzergrenadier divisions were motorised infantry divisions issued with armoured and semi-armoured vehicles to enable them to move and fight with the panzer divisions. The basic difference between the panzer and panzergrenadier formations was that the former was stronger in numbers of tanks. Both types

25th Panzer

3rd Panzergrenadier

Panzer Division
Feldherrnhalle

22nd Motorised Infantry Division

1st SS-Panzer Division

2nd SS-Panzer Division

26th Panzer

10th Panzergrenadier

25th Panzergrenadier

3rd SS-Panzer Division

14th Motorised Infantry Division

29th Panzergrenadier

4th SS-Panzergrenadier
Division

27th Panzer

16th Panzergrenadier

36th Motorised Infantry Division

5th SS-Panzer Division

116th Panzer

18th Panzergrenadier

60th Motorised Infantry Division

9th SS-Panzer Division

Lehr Division

20th Panzergrenadier

Grossdeutschland Division

10th SS-Panzer Division

11th SS-Panzergrenadier
Division

of divisions had two battalions of infantry but while the panzer division had a regiment (three battalions) of tanks, the panzergrenadier division had only one battalion.

Units detailed in the following panzergrenadier divisions are those which were allocated to the divisions in 1944-45.

3rd Panzergrenadier
(Based on IIIrd Military District, Berlin)
Panzergrenadier Regiments 8, 28
Panzer Battalion 103
Artillery Regiment 3
Panzer Aufkl Abt 103

10th Panzergrenadier
(Based on the XIIIth Military District, Nuremberg)
Panzergrenadier Regiments 20, 41
Panzer Battalion 7
Artillery Regiment 10
Panzer Aufkl Abt 110

14th Motorised Infantry Division
Grenadier Regiments 11, 53
Panzer Aufkl Abt 114
(Note that this regiment, like the 22nd and 36th Motorised Infantry Divisions, had no integral tank battalion or artillery regiment)

16th Panzergrenadier
(Based on the VIth Military District Münster)
Panzergrenadier Regiments 60, 156
Panzer Battalion 116
Artillery Regiment 146
Panzer Aufkl Abt 116

18th Panzergrenadier
(Based on VIIIth Military District, Breslau)
Panzergrenadier Regiments (Motorised) 30, 51
Panzer Battalion 118
Artillery Regiment 118
Panzer Aufkl Abt 118

20th Panzergrenadier
(Based on Xth Military District, Hamburg)
Panzergrenadier Regiments 76, 90
Panzer Battalion 8
Artillery Regiment 20
Panzer Aufkl Abt 120

Panzergrenadier Division Feldherrnhalle
(Based on the XXth Military district, Danzig)
This division listed on page 141 is shown as both a panzer division and a panzergrenadier division in Wehrmacht Orders of Battle.
Composed of:
Panzergrenadier Regiment FHH
Panzer Füselier Regiment FHH
Panzer Battalion FHH
Artillery Regiment FHH
Panzer Aufkl Abt FHH

Its establishment was in fact that of a panzergrenadier division.

22nd Motorised Infantry Division
This division whose major combat units were the 16th and 65th Grenadier Regiments and No 122 Reconnaissance Units was under-established as a panzergrenadier regiment.

25th Panzergrenadier
(Based on Vth Military District, Stuttgart)
Panzergrenadier Regiments 35, 119
Panzer Battalion 5
Artillery Regiment 25
Panzer Aufkl Abt 126

29th Panzergrenadier
(Based on IXth Military District, Kassel)
Panzergrenadier Regiments 15, 71
Panzer Battalion 129
Artillery Regiment 29
Panzer Aufkl Abt 129

36th Motorised Infantry Division
(Similar in establishment to the 14th and 22nd Motorised Inf. Div.)
Grenadier Regiments 87, 118
Panzer Aufkl Abt 136

60th Motorised Infantry Division
(Based on XXth Military District, Danzig)
Motorised Grenadier Regiments 92, 120
Panzer Battalion 160
Artillery Regiment 160
Panzer Aufkl Abt 160

Panzergrenadier Division 'Grossdeutschland'
Mention of the élite *Grossdeutschland* Division has been made on page 141. In 1944 when it was fighting in Bessarabia the "GD's" major combat units were:
Panzergrenadier Regiment *'Grossdeutschland'*
Panzer Fuselier Regiment *'Grossdeutschland'*
Panzer Regiment *'Grossdeutschland'*
Artillery Regiment *'Grossdeutschland'*
Panzer Aufkl Abt *'Grossdeutschland'*

One battalion of the Panzergrenadier Regiment GD, and one battalion of the Fuselier Regiment GD was transported in armoured troop carriers, the other two battalions of both regiments were motorised. Both regiments had their own integral anti-tank, anti-aircraft and self-propelled artillery units. One battalion of the Panzer Regiment GD was equipped with PzKpfw V Panther tanks; another with PzKpfw IV tanks; and the third battalion with PzKpfw VI Tiger tanks.

Towards the end of the war a number of specialised élite motorised and armoured units were grouped together under the collective title *'Grossdeutschland Verbände'* and wearing *Grossdeutschland* insignia and 'GD' badges on their sleeves.

These units included the *Führer-Begleit-Division* — a formation of divisional strength which had been raised in 1939 as a motorised escort battalion (the *Führer-Begleit-Battalion*). (The division was annihilated on the Eastern front in April 1945. At that time it was organised as a conventional panzer division.)

Another similar unit was the *Führer-Grenadier-Division,* orginally raised in 1944 after the attempt on Hitler's life as a special headquarters protection brigade.)

Panzergrenadier Brigades

Within the panzergrenadier division the two panzergrenadier regiments — infantry regiments normally of two *Abteilungen* (battalions) each were known as a panzergrenadier brigade. Independent panzergrenadier brigades with a similar or augmented establishment also existed, and in the summer of 1944 the German High Command ordered the formation of thirteen independent panzer brigades. These were to be numbered 101-113. Although the brigades were formed few of them ever reached full strength and none actually saw service in an independent role — their units being absorbed by panzer divisions needing reinforcements.

Panzer and Panzergrenadier Divisions of the Waffen-SS

All the SS-Panzer Divisions and SS-Panzergrenadier Divisions were formed from motorised SS-Infantry Divisions. The original SS-Divisions earned a reputation as extremely good fighting troops and after their successes round Kharkov in March 1943 their establishment was increased to convert them to full panzer divisions.

1st SS-Panzer Division ('The *Leibstandarte Adolf Hitler*')
Formed from the Führer's bodyguard troops.
SS-Panzergrenadier Regiments 1 and 2
SS-Panzer Regiment 1
SS-Panzer Artillery Regiment 1
2nd SS-Panzer Division ('*Das Reich*')
SS-Panzergrenadier Regiments 3 and 4
SS-Panzer Regiment 2
SS-Panzer Artillery Regiment 2
3rd SS-Panzer Division ('*Totenkopf*')
SS-Panzergrenadier Regiment 5 and 6
SS-Panzer Regiment 3
SS-Panzer Artillery Regiment 3
4th SS-Panzergrenadier Division (*Polizei*) Disbanded in 1942
Polizei-Panzergrenadier Regiments 7 and 8
SS-Panzer Battalion 4
SS-Panzer Artillery Regiment 4

5th SS-Panzer Division (*Wiking*)
SS-Panzergrenadier Regiments 9 and 10
SS-Panzer Regiment 5
SS-Panzer Artillery Regiment 5
9th SS-Panzer Division (*Hohenstaufen*)
SS-Panzergrenadier Regiments 19 and 20
SS-Panzer Regiment 9
SS-Panzer Artillery Regiment 9
10th SS-Panzer Division (*Frundsberg*)
SS-Panzergrenadier Regiments 21 and 22
SS-Panzer Regiment 10
SS-Panzer Artillery Regiment 10
11th SS-Panzergrenadier Division (*Nordland*)
SS-Panzergrenadier Regiments 23 and 24
SS-Panzer Battalion 11.
SS-Panzer Artillery Regiment 11

Foreign Nazi sympathisers who 'volunteered' for service with the German army were used to fill up élite SS units and to form *Freiwillige* (volunteer) units. The *Wiking* (5th SS-Panzer division) the *Nordland* (11th SS-Panzergrenadiers) the *Handschar* (13th Waffen Gebirgsdivision) and two Waffen-SS Grenadier Divisions (the 14th *Galiz I* and 15th *Lett I*) all had large numbers of non-German volunteers at one time. Poor performance in battle, largely due to language problems, resulted in the disbandment in 1943 of all but the *Nordland* Panzergrenadier Division into which the best of the *Freiwilligen* were combined.

12th SS-Panzer Division (*Hitler Jugend*)
SS-Panzergrenadier Regiments 25 and 26
SS-Panzer Regiment 12
SS-Panzer Artillery Regiment 12
The troops in this division were recruited mainly from the Nazi Youth Movement.

Miscellaneous Formations which included Panzer Units

Two SS-Cavalry divisions (the *8th Kavallerie* and the 22nd *Freiwillige Kavallerie der SS*) which saw considerable service had panzer units either integral or attached to them at some time or other. Other divisions, such as the 16th (*Reichsführer* SS), 17th (*Götz von Berlichingen*) and 18th (*Horst Wessel*) Panzergrenadier Division were regular panzer formations, although the personnel were mainly aliens — mostly Volksdeutsche, German individuals from the occupied territories. Other formations like the 23rd Waffen-Grenadier Division der SS (*Kama*), the 32nd SS-Panzer Division (*30 Januar*) formed in 1945 from troops in training establishments, and the 38th SS-Panzergrenadier Division (*Nibelungen*) which was formed in 1945 partly from the staff of the officers school at Bad Tölz, existed mainly on paper.